A
Leader's
Legacy

A Leader's Legacy

James M. Kouzes
Barry Z. Posner

JOSSEY-BASS
A Wiley Imprint
www.josseybass.com

Published by Jossey-Bass
A Wiley Imprint
989 Market Street, San Francisco, CA 94103-1741 www.josseybass.com

Jossey-Bass books and products are available through most bookstores. To contact Jossey-Bass directly call our Customer Care Department within the U.S. at 800-956-7739, outside the U.S. at 317-572-3986, or fax 317-572-4002.

Jossey-Bass also publishes its books in a variety of electronic formats. Some content that appears in print may not be available in electronic books.

Library of Congress Cataloging-in-Publication Data

Kouzes, James M., 1945-
　　A leader's legacy / James M. Kouzes, Barry Z. Posner.
　　　　p. cm.
　　Includes bibliographical references and index.
　　ISBN-13: 978-0-7879-8296-6 (cloth)
　　ISBN-10: 0-7879-8296-2 (cloth)
　　1. Leadership.   I. Posner, Barry Z.   II. Title.
　　HD57.7.K6798 2006
　　658.4'092—dc22

　　　　　　　　　　　　　　　　　　2006015687

Printed in the United States of America
FIRST EDITION
HB Printing　10 9 8 7 6 5 4 3

Contents

v

CONTENTS

PART THREE   Aspirations   89

PART FOUR   Courage   131

Introduction

This book began its life as a response to a challenge from our editor, Susan Williams. She wanted us to write a book that was "a free-flowing exploration of leadership topics and lessons" that we'd learned over two decades of studying, researching, writing, talking, and consulting on this theme. She wanted us to wrestle with the "paradoxes, conundrums, burning issues, and ambiguous questions" that those who'd been in the trenches might ponder. She cajoled us to "come down from the podium" and to be "much more personal, introspective, subtler, and at times, more blunt" in our writing style.

We weren't altogether sure we could accomplish what Susan wanted. We weren't even sure we knew what she meant by a lot of what she said. But we accepted her challenge and set off. We soon learned that after nearly twenty-five years of writing together, doing something differently was not an easy assignment. We should have known this, given how often we've advised others that changing the way you do things requires hard work and some heartache.

We started out by identifying the questions we were constantly asked about leaders, leading, and leadership, and we recorded our observations of the things we've learned over the years. We had touched on some of these themes in our other books, but mainly our goal was to open some new territory and chart some new pathways in our exploration of the bigger issues around leading. However, what was supposed to be a free-flowing exploration of a topic was littered by the debris of past expeditions.

We had made a list of essays that we considered writing, but the collection resembled Christmas ornaments strewn randomly on the ground. Each one looked nice, but we had no tree to hang them on: no central theme to help us pull everything together. Then we had an epiphany that helped us to connect the dots. In a conversation with Tae Moon Kouzes, Jim's wife and an executive coach, we were agonizing over our dilemma. We shared with her the list of essays, and one of them was "The Legacy You Leave Is the Life You Lead," which later became the Afterword for this book. Tae liked that title a lot, she said, adding, "Every leader I've ever worked with wants to leave a legacy." Her comment struck a chord.

We began to reflect on the possibility that "legacy" could, in fact, be the right organizing framework for the entire book, not just for one essay.

We had quite a debate between ourselves about the legacy idea at first. We weren't entirely sure every leader *wanted* to leave a legacy, though we were quite sure leaders left one in spite of themselves. We also didn't want to paint ourselves into a tautological corner by assuming that every decision a leader made was a legacy-based decision.

We were even more concerned that making the statement that every leader wants to leave a legacy would link leadership to a position or place in the organization rather than to the perspective that everyone, regardless of position, can make a difference. It's been our contention all along that leadership is everyone's business, and that all of us have the capacity to, as the familiar camping dictum instructs, "leave the campsite a little better than you found it."

Moreover, it was somewhat troubling to think that leaders would be constantly wondering, "What's my legacy going to be if I do this?" instead of doing what they think is proper with the knowledge that history will judge whether or not their contributions are worthy of being remembered. Being self-absorbed in one's legacy seemed counter to the notion that leaders are selfless.

Back and forth we went, but in the end we came to see how the legacy theme ran through the majority of the lessons we'd learned over the years. It is represented best in what Gail Mayville, whose leadership we wrote about many years ago, said when asked why she stepped forward and took action: "For me, personally, I am driven by the legacy I am leaving my children." We all may not be as conscious as Gail was about her choices, but we ought to be. For if we were, we might be leaving the kind of legacy we want to leave instead of an accidental and unintended one.

In addition, thinking about a legacy can be extremely energizing and uplifting. It forces us to think about today's actions in a larger context. It requires an appreciation of others. None of us are the sole inhabitants of our organizations or our communities—we do not live alone. It requires us to take responsibility for our own actions with a realization that they will always have consequences, if not immediately, then for sure in the future. The legacy perspective explicitly reveals that we make a difference. Then the only question remaining to consider is, What kind of difference do I want to make?

There's nothing inherently contradictory about asking leaders to think about their personal legacies and asking them to focus on others' contributions. There's nothing inherently selfish in thinking about our legacies, anymore than there's something inherently selfish in thinking about our visions and values. We know from our research that the people who are clearest about their vision and values are significantly more committed to their organizations than are those who are not clear about their vision and values. While we don't have the same hard evidence about legacy, we would hypothesize that clarity about legacy produces the same results.

Thinking about our legacies requires us to move beyond short-term definitions of success. Legacies encompass past, present, and future, and when pondering our legacies we're forced to consider where we've been, where we are now, and where we're going. We're brought face-to-face with questions of who we are and why we're here. We have to consider more deeply the true value of what was, what is, and what will be. We search our souls for the deeper meaning in our lives. A heartfelt quest to leave a lasting legacy is a journey from success to significance.

We all have choices in our lives. One choice is to say "Hey, I'm here only for me, so I won't bother to clean up the campsite or put out the fire. What the heck, I won't be back here again, so why should I care?" Another is to say, "Those who follow me will want to enjoy this beautiful campsite. What can I do to ensure that their experience will be even better than mine?"

Being clear that we want to leave the campsite better than we found it compels us to take actions that make it better. Legacy thinking means dedicating ourselves to *making a difference,* not just working to achieve fame and fortune. It also means appreciating that others will inherit what we leave behind.

By asking ourselves how we want to be remembered, we plant the seeds for living our lives as if we matter. By living each day as if we matter, we offer up our own unique legacy. By offering up our own unique legacy, we make the world we inhabit a better place than we found it.

This book offers twenty-one essays grouped together in four sections—plus the Afterword—that represent some of our thoughts on legacy: Significance, Relationships, Aspirations, and Courage. The essays are brief and to the point. They represent brand new experiences and stories as well as new variations on familiar themes. We hope that they will stimulate and challenge you to explore the choices you make as you walk your path to greatness.

PART ONE

Significance

hen we move on, people do not remember us for what we do for ourselves. They remember us for what we do for them. They are the inheritors of our work. One of the great joys and grave responsibilities of leaders is making sure that those in their care live lives not only of success but also of significance.

Exemplary leaders are interested more in others' success than in their own. Their greatest achievements are the triumphs of those they serve. Knowing they have made a difference in others' lives is what motivates their own, giving leaders the strength to endure the hardships, struggles, and inevitable sacrifices required to achieve great things. Leaders who see their role as serving others leave the most lasting legacies.

Teaching is one way of serving. It's a way of passing along the lessons learned from experience. The best leaders are teachers. The best teachers are also the best learners. They know that by investing in developing others they are also developing themselves.

Learning requires feedback. When leaders ask, "How am I doing?" they gain valuable insights into how they affect the performance of others. The trouble is that most leaders don't ask. It's one of the most glaring leadership shortcomings, and one that desperately needs to be overcome. The best leaders know they can't possibly be perfect, so they embrace their "loving critics"—those people who care so much that they're willing to tell their leaders the truth.

Speaking of the truth, for each individual, the most important leader in any organization is *not* the CEO or the head honcho; it's the leader we see most often, the one we turn to when we need guidance and support. Whether your title is manager, team leader, coach, teacher, principal, doctor, director, or parent, *you* are the most important leader in your organization for the people who look to you.

Even so, in leadership and in life nothing that we accomplish is singular. No one ever got anything extraordinary done alone. A leader's legacy is the legacy of many, and none of those who contribute to making a difference want to be taken for granted. No one likes to be an assumption. Everyone wants to be significant.

CHAPTER 1 | Leaders Serve and Sacrifice

Are you on this planet to do something, or are you here just for something to do? If you're on this planet to do something, then what is it? What difference will you make? What will be your legacy?

We pose these questions to first-year students in our leadership classes at Santa Clara University. It's pretty heady stuff for eighteen-year-olds barely three months out of high school. Most adults haven't thought seriously enough about these questions. We don't expect our students to have ready responses. We just believe that they ought to be thinking about what their legacies will be— not only as they begin their college careers but throughout all the days of their lives.

"What will be your legacy?" does not have a single answer or a right answer. It's not like a math problem with a formula we can offer. But asking the question opens our students to the notion that along life's journey they're going to be struggling with determining the difference they want to make, and with doing things that matter. They're going to be making choices at school, at work, at home, and in the community, and every choice they make will be part of the legacy they leave, however consciously or unconsciously they behave.

Asking the question about legacy brings forward another central observation: leadership is not solely about producing results. Success in leadership is not measured only in numbers. Being a leader brings with it a responsibility to do something of significance that makes families, communities, work organizations, nations, the environment, and the world better places than they are today. Not all these things can be quantified.

Our own studies, as well as those of many other authors and scholars who have explored leadership and leaders, have shown that leadership often begins with pain and suffering (our own and in the conditions of others). Our colleague Patrick Lencioni, the author of several best-selling leadership books, told us that when he graduated from college he "wanted to change the world. Call it what you will, I was determined to make a difference." However, the problem with this zeal, he went on to explain, was that he hadn't thought deeply enough about two fundamental matters: "Who are the people I am really serving? And am I ready to suffer?"

Each of us has to answer these questions of ourselves before we can change the world, make a difference, and leave a legacy. If we're going to be authentic in our leadership, we have to be willing to serve, and we have to be willing to suffer.

"Now, wait a minute," you say. "Do you mean to tell me that I have to work hard all my life, and that when I get to be a leader what I get in return is that I have to serve others and I have to suffer in the process? That's not what I signed up for. No one ever told me that leaders have to do *that!*"

Only Leaders Who Serve Earn Commitment

Everything leaders do is about providing service.

Our late colleague John Gardner once observed, "A loyal constituency is won when the people, consciously or unconsciously, judge the leader to be capable of solving their problems and meeting their needs."[1] (John knew a lot about leadership, having once been Secretary of Health, Education and Welfare, founded Common Cause, and served as an adviser to six U.S. presidents, as well as being a respected author and scholar.) John didn't mean that the leader should personally fix the problems and fulfill the needs. What he was suggesting is that people willingly follow someone who's attuned to their aspirations, fears, and ideals. Loyalty is not something a boss can demand. It's something people choose to grant to a person who has earned it. The people's choice to follow is based not simply upon authority but upon the leader's perceived capacity to meet a need.

Perhaps we can better present the importance of the constituent perspective by rephrasing John's comment. Try reading it this way: "Loyal *customers* are won when the *customers,* consciously or unconsciously, judge the *company* to be capable of solving their problems and meeting their needs." Isn't that exactly how organizations win customer loyalty? By solving problems and meeting needs? Customers decide whether to continue to give us their business, and if we want our customers' loyalty then it's our job to be responsive.

The same is true for leaders. Constituents decide whether or not they'll be loyal. Loyalty is earned when constituents decide that their needs are getting met, so leaders who want commitment had better see their jobs as requiring responsiveness. Believing foremost in service means being more concerned about the welfare of others than you are about your own well-being.

Now, the first objection we always hear to this point of view is that customers pay us, but we pay our followers. Oh, really? That might be true if the only constituents you thought you had were your employees, *and* if all you were considering was the paycheck. But what about energy, drive, initiative, spirit, dedication, and all the other emotional currencies that people pay us with? And what about your peers, your suppliers, your business partners, and the like? Aren't they also your constituents?

When we talked to Betsy Sanders, who at the time was general manager for Nordstrom in California, she was quite emphatic about this point. "I serve my associates so that they can serve our customers well. Actually, I'm at the bottom of the organizational pyramid supporting them and not at the top with them supporting me." When leaders accept that they are servants first, then they clearly know where they stand. And it's not at the head of the line.

Viewing leadership as service is not a new concept. More than three decades ago Robert Greenleaf, himself a retired corporate executive, observed that the "great leader is seen as servant first, and that simple fact is the key to [the leader's] greatness."[2] We release tremendous power and energy when we serve. Nancy Ortberg, former teaching pastor at Willow Creek Church and now a church leadership consultant, pointed it out to us this way:

> Without the element of servant leadership, the furthest you will get into someone's motivation is the *"have to"* level. Over time, that will build a narrow, thin organization. When a leader is able to drive down deep and get to the *"I want"* motivation, the organization becomes a type of perpetual motion machine. It no longer takes

as much energy from you as a leader because you've built into those around you the zeal to do a job well. The "sustain" you've tapped in your team will carry all of you, collectively, well into the future.

The purpose of leaders is to mobilize others to serve a purpose. And if you're here to serve a purpose, the purpose comes first. You'll have to make sacrifices in service of that purpose. In this age of reality shows like *Survivor, The Apprentice,* and *The Amazing Race* it might appear to some that success is winner-take-all and at all costs. Not to us, not to our students, not to Pat Lencioni, not to John Gardner, not to Robert Greenleaf, and not to Nancy Ortberg.

Passionate Leaders Are Willing to Suffer

When people talk about leadership, they often use the word *passion.* And when we think about passion we tend to think of emotions like enthusiasm, zeal, energy, exuberance, and intensity. Well, all these attributions might be true, but when you look up the word *passion* in any dictionary that includes origins you'll see that it comes from the Latin word for *suffering.* Passion is suffering! A passionate person is someone who suffers and a *compas-sionate* person is someone who suffers with, and shares the suffering of, others—and wants to take action to alleviate this condition. Nearly every act of leadership requires suffering—and often for the leader a choice between one's personal success and safety and the greater welfare of others. We're asking you to understand that nothing great comes without costs.

Leadership is hard work. It's not easy despite what we, or others, may write in our attempts to make leadership more accessible. While we offer words of encouragement, tools and techniques, examples, and practical applications with the hope of improving leadership skills and confidence, we fully recognize that nothing great was ever accomplished without making sacrifices. At times we will suffer, and those we love and cherish will suffer, if only because of the trade-offs we have to make between our own personal interests and those of the greater good. If you want to be a leader, you must be willing to pay a price. By sacrificing, you demonstrate that you're *not* in it for yourself. This sends the message, loud and clear, that you have the best interests of others at heart.

The most significant contributions leaders make are not to today's bottom line but to the long-term development of individuals and institutions that adapt, prosper, and grow. People should never take on the job of leadership if they're unwilling to see beyond their own needs. If they do, they will ultimately fail.

We'll all be remembered for something. The question is, for what? What will others say about you when you're no longer around? Each of us lives on in the memories we create, in the systems and practices we set in place (or don't), and in the lives we touch. We guarantee that what people will say about you will not be about what you achieved for yourself but what you achieved for others. Not how big a campfire you built but how well you kept others warm, how well you illuminated the night to make them feel safe, and how beautiful you left the campsite for those who would come after you to build the next fire.

CHAPTER 2

The Best Leaders Are Teachers

We've been fortunate in our careers to work with some of the most seasoned professionals in leadership and human resources development. One of them is Fred Margolis. Fred taught us one lesson in particular that has shaped much of what we've done as educators.

Over the course of a dinner one evening, Fred asked, "What's the best way to learn something?" Since we'd had extensive training and background in experiential learning—and had personal preferences for that approach—we confidently replied: "The best way to learn something is to experience it yourself."

"No," Fred responded instantly, as if he'd sensed we were going to give the answer we did. "The *best* way to learn something," he told us, "is to teach it to somebody else!"

That was one of those moments when your brain does a double take, and you realize that you've just heard something extremely profound and a whole new world is about to unfold. What we learned from Fred that evening continues to benefit us to this day. We've gained at least two lessons from that experience. The first is the obvious one—the best way to learn something is to teach it to somebody else. The second lesson came to us more recently as a blinding flash of the obvious when we realized that legacies are passed on in the stories we tell.

Lesson One: The Best Way to Learn Is to Teach

No matter whether you're a leader or a new recruit, a veteran or a novice, a teacher or a student, if you're really serious about helping others learn, you start to think, study, and prepare from the moment you're asked to take on that role. In the process you become consumed by learning. You know you're on the line. You know you're going to have to perform live in front of others, and you'd better have your stuff down cold.

The lesson that *the best way to learn something is to teach it to somebody else* has shaped our teaching style more significantly than any other lesson on learning. It's Fred's legacy, and we've been benefiting from it and passing it on ever since dinner that night. It inspires us daily to discover new methods, invent new tools, and design new experiences that will enable others to grow and develop.

Even when we're asked to give a lecture on something we know by heart—after all, we are hired because we're the subject matter experts—we always try to provide an opportunity for participants to become the teachers. It could be as simple as asking them a question or having them offer an example from their own experience. When they have to talk to even one other person about their own experiences or have to speak to the entire audience about an opinion they might have, they've got to reach deeper inside than if we just leave them to sit there passively and listen.

This same principle applies to leadership. As the late Peter Drucker observed early in his career:

> People learn the most when teaching others. My third employer was the youngest of three senior partners of a bank. . . . Once a week or so he would sit down with me and talk about the way he saw the world. . . . He used me as an audience, and in the process he demonstrated how to think. He talked about the same subject over and over again until it clicked. . . . In the end, I think he learned more than I did from our little talks.[1]

As Peter implies, one of the things that leaders do is to mentor and teach. And when they're teaching, at least with the intensity of Peter's early employer, they're learning. Not all leaders see it this way, but the very best do. Each and every interaction you have with your associates can be framed as a learning opportunity for them—and for you.

Take a performance appraisal, for example. You can view it as a perfunctory exercise in describing someone's scores on certain measures and competencies, or you can look at it as a mutual learning opportunity. These sessions become mutual learning opportunities when you approach them as chances for people to *teach you* about their strengths, weaknesses, aspirations, goals, disappointments, confusions, vulnerabilities, and the like. They become mutual learning opportunities when you approach them as chances for you *to teach* your associates about your own struggles with these issues and what you've learned from your experience, and for them to *teach you* about the same. It transforms the experience from a monologue to a dialogue. It also elevates your relationships from boss-subordinate to mentor-protégé.

Imagine you're that mentor who sits down once a week and has a conversation about the way you see the world, just as Peter Drucker's did. Imagine talking about the vexing issues of the day. Imagine that you're engaged in such a way that you're not only teaching but also learning. If you were to approach every serious interaction this way, chances are you'd be asking as many questions as you gave answers. ("So, what do you think?") Chances are you'd be listening as much as you were telling. ("If I heard you correctly, you're saying that . . . ") Chances are you'd become a student yourself, and those who were with you would come away feeling they'd helped to teach you something. ("Now, that's interesting. I'd never quite thought about it that way.") Imagine how extraordinarily powerful these kinds of interactions would be.

One of the most powerful legacies you can leave is to turn every person you lead, whether a manager or an individual contributor, into a teacher. When they become fully engaged in the experience of *learning*—not just the experience of doing—people will realize a benefit that extends far beyond the production of a quality product or the performance of exemplary service. They will realize that within them is unused capacity and untapped potential. They will experience the magic of self-discovery. They will experience the great joy that comes with the realization, "I can do it!" And when you and your colleagues experience that kind of profound knowledge, there is nothing you can't accomplish.

Lesson Two: Legacies Are Passed on in the Stories We Tell

The second lesson from this experience came to us as we began thinking about the theme of legacy for this book. It occurred to us that *our teachers continue to teach as we go on to tell their stories.*

The story of Fred is just one of the hundreds of stories we tell. Up until recently when recounting the story we had only thought about the obvious lesson we were teaching—the moral of the story, so to speak. But now, something else strikes us as we relate the story about that dinner with Fred: as we've recounted this story to thousands of people over the years, Fred continues to teach us and to teach others who've never met him. But not only that. The story we tell is passing along Fred's legacy to us. The same can be said for the legacies of all the other people whose stories we tell—and whose stories you tell.

Each of us, whether we intend to or not, will become at some point a character in someone's story. We all talk about people when they're not around, and others will talk about us when we're not around. The obvious question is, What will they say?

This should make each of us wonder about a few things.

- What lessons am I teaching in each interaction I have? The "moral of the story" may be obvious, but what else am I teaching? Am I even aware of it?
- What stories will others tell about me in the future? What will others learn from those stories? What's the legacy that's being passed along? What's the legacy I want to pass along?

• What am I learning from others as I teach?

Put all this together with something we discovered when analyzing the teaching evaluations that students have filled out over the years at the Leavey School of Business, Santa Clara University. We found that the most highly rated teachers are those who are most enthusiastic about their material.

This squares directly with your own experience, doesn't it? When you're in class with someone who's truly passionate about their subject matter, don't you get jazzed about it? Don't they really turn you on to the subject? Don't you wish all your teachers could be this way?

The same thing applies to leaders. The best leaders are the most passionate about their work, their organizations, and their disciplines. Their enthusiasm is contagious, and others catch that enthusiasm and display it in their own work. We wish all our leaders could be this excited. These are the leaders we will tell the most positive stories about in the future. These are the leaders who continue to make a difference long after we, and they, have moved on.

There are only two reasons great teachers know more than their students, and great leaders know more than their constituents. One, they've dedicated themselves to learning. Two, they love what they're learning. Come to think of it, maybe that's just one reason.

CHAPTER 3

We All Need Loving Critics

The late John Gardner, leadership scholar and presidential adviser, once remarked, "Pity the leader caught between unloving critics and uncritical lovers." We're quite taken by this observation. It should be on a poster that hangs over every leader's desk—or a screen saver on every leader's computer—and it should be read and contemplated several times a day.

None of us likes to hear the constant screeching of harpies who have only foul things to say. We close our ears to constant complainers who are predictable in their whining. At the same time, we never benefit from, nor truly believe, the sycophants whose flattery is obviously aimed at gaining favor. We know that no one can be that good. To stay honest with ourselves, what we really need are "loving critics"—people who care deeply enough to give us honest feedback about how we're doing.

The problem is that most leaders don't want honest feedback, don't ask for honest feedback, and don't get much of it unless it's forced on them. At least that's what we've discovered in our research.

In our most recent analysis of data from more than seventy thousand individuals who completed the *Leadership Practices Inventory,* our thirty-item behavioral assessment, we've found that the statement that ranks lowest from the observers' perspective, and next to lowest from the leaders' perspective, is this one:

> 16. (He or she) asks for feedback on how his/her actions affect other people's performance.

When we related this finding to the director of leadership development for one of the world's largest technology companies, he told us that the same was true for his organization. The lowest-scoring item on its internal leadership assessment was the one on seeking feedback.

Further validation comes when we ask executive coaches, "How many of your clients begin their coaching sessions with you by asking, 'How am I doing?'" The most common answer: "None." The higher up you go on the corporate ladder, the less likely it is that leaders will ask for feedback. Leaders want to know how others are doing, but rarely do they ask how they are doing. Senior executives are quite happy to prescribe 360-degree feedback for others; it's all the rage these days. But when it comes to getting it, it's not for them. And if they're getting it, it's probably because an outside consultant or coach told them they should be getting it, not because they took the initiative to ask.

Let's think about this for a moment. Credibility, which is at the foundation of leadership, from a *behavioral* perspective is about doing what you say you will do. But how can you do what you say if you don't know how you're doing? If you never ask for feedback on your behavior and on how your behavior affects how others are doing, how can you really expect to align your words and your actions over the long haul?

There's solid evidence that the best leaders are highly attuned to what's going on inside themselves as they are leading and to what's going on with others. They're very self-aware and they're very socially aware. They can tell in short order whether they've done something that has enabled someone to perform at a higher level or whether they've sent motivation heading south.

Think about it this way. One morning you're in your car on the way to work. You glance at your dashboard and notice the water temperature gauge indicates that your engine is running a little hot. You say to yourself, "Hmmm," and continue driving. Halfway to work you smell something odd coming through your vents, and wonder to yourself, "What's that odor?" Still, you keep on driving. A few moments later steam is rising from under the hood, so you pull over, raise the hood, and, sure enough, your engine has overheated. You call the roadside repair service, have your car towed to the shop, and miss half a day of work. Looking back, you realize you had early warning signals of a problem, but you chose to keep on driving.

The same is true in leading. Paying attention to the early warnings prevents more serious problems later. Setting up a system for getting regular feedback (the equivalent of the dashboard) and *paying attention* to that feedback will help you move the organization forward more effectively. All leaders want to have a positive impact on performance. It's part of their legacy. The only way they can know if they're having the desired impact is to get regular feedback on how they're doing. Leaders need more loving critics.

Yet our data and experience tell us that leaders don't seem to *want* honest feedback. It's typically treated like an unwanted pest at a party. Why is that? Why do they not want something that has so many personal, professional, and organizational benefits?

Author Ralph Keyes offers this insight in *The Courage to Write:* "As author-editors discover, all the other anxieties—the many courage points of the writing process—are merely stretching exercises for the big one: feeling *exposed* (in every sense of the word)."[1] He goes on to tell about how one author friend of his "compared writing novels to dancing naked on a table."

It seems to us that the same thing is true for leaders. The reason why leaders aren't eager to ask for feedback is they are afraid of feeling exposed. Exposed as not being perfect, as not knowing everything, as not being as good at leadership as they should be, as not being up to the task.

Our friend and colleague Dan Mulhern offers us a related perspective. Dan is the First Gentleman of the State of Michigan—yes, his wife is the governor. As part of a workshop he asked fifteen people who regularly observe his work to give him an assessment of how he was doing. He received both quantitative data and some verbatim comments on his strengths and areas for improvement. The feedback was anonymous.

While the suggestions he received were informative, they made him wonder. "Why hadn't anyone told me?" he asked. "Why did they *need* the cover of anonymity?"[2]

Dan offered this observation:

> To me this is the lesson: it is *hard* to get good feedback. The default position in our cultures is: fear. Fear of getting honest feedback (I had some), and probably even more fear of giving it. Fear of retribution. Fear of hurting someone's feelings. Face it; authorities didn't use to ask for feedback. Parents didn't want to hear it. Siblings sure as heck didn't. Teachers hardly did. There just aren't a lot of people who model seeking and giving constructive feedback. So, in our normal lives at work,

people who could be helping us understand how to help them be more effective, and how to lead in ways that work, just don't tell us.

There you have it. The two sides of the coin. On the one side you see the leader fearing exposure. On the other you see a group of colleagues who fear retribution or hurting someone. Well, you know what? If you're the leader you're already dancing naked on the table, so no use pretending you're wearing clothes.

It seems to us that the better strategy is for all of us to accept the importance of seeking feedback about our performance. Learning to be a better leader requires great self-awareness and it requires making ourselves vulnerable. Make sure you have processes for getting regular feedback. As Dan says, "If you want feedback, you have to work to get it."

In addition to the annual 360-degree assessment, try this the next time you're in a meeting. Begin by asking, "How am I doing?" More than likely you'll be greeted with stunned silence—a sure sign folks are not used to being asked this question by you (or anyone else) and are uncomfortable in responding. But if you wait long enough some brave soul may venture an honest response. When that happens, immediately recognize the speaker for showing some courage, and tell the rest of the group, "That's what we need more of around here. More loving critics."

CHAPTER 4

You Are the Most Important Leader in Your Organization

The CEO is not the most important leader in an organization—unless, of course, you happen to report directly to that person. Despite the fact that CEOs get most of the press, they get far too much credit for the successes and far too much blame for the failures of organizations. The attributions are way out of proportion to their actual influence.

If the CEO isn't the most important leader, then who is? Well, if you're a manager in an organization, to your direct reports *you* are the most important leader in your organization. You are more likely than any other leader to influence whether people will stay, perform at their best, wow customers, or be motivated to share the organization's vision and values. In other words, you are the CEO of your group.

Lots of evidence supports this claim. Consider just these three items from among the many we could cite:

- When asked to identify the category from which they'd most likely choose a leadership role model, young people select "family members" as their number one choice. This is followed by teachers and coaches and then community leaders. When asked the same question, middle-aged managers select business leaders, followed by family members and then teachers and coaches.
- Longitudinal studies of corporate executives reveal that the single best predictor of career success is the relationship they had with their very first supervisor. The character and quality of that relationship—for example, the expectations that your first supervisor had about your work potential—are more important than where you went to school, what grades you got, what you studied, who your parents were, what field or industry you were in, and the like.
- When asked what contributes most to ethical behavior in your organization, the most frequent response from employees—managers and individual contributors at every hierarchical level— is "the behavior of my boss." When asked what contributes most to *un*ethical behavior in your

organization, the most frequent response is identical—"the behavior of my boss."

Reflect on these findings for a moment. What do you notice? What's the underlying message here? When we ask participants in our leadership programs to share their observations, invariably one thing becomes very apparent: The leaders who have the most influence on us are those who are closest to us.

When we're young, we're more likely to view our parents, teachers, and coaches, or people in the local community, as potential leadership role models. Why is this? Probably because we have more daily contact with them than we do with other possible role models. These are the folks we look to as examples of what leaders should or should not do.

When we're out of school and at our workplaces we're more likely to select business leaders first, because we have more regular contact with them than with others. But even among adults, family members and teachers and coaches closely follow business leaders as leadership role models. Our early influencers never really disappear from our consciousness.

When at work—whether in the executive suite, the retail shop, the factory floor, the back room, a field operation, or the corporate headquarters—the person most likely to influence our performance, positively or negatively, is our most immediate manager. That person is most likely to influence the trajectory of our careers, our ethical behavior, and our satisfaction with our jobs.

If you're a parent, teacher, coach, or community leader, *you* are the person setting the example for young people. It's not hip-hop artists, movie stars, professional athletes, or the president of the United States they look to for guidance on leadership. You are the one they are most likely going to look to for how a leader responds to competitive situations, or handles crises, or deals with loss, or resolves ethical dilemmas. It's not someone else. It's you.

Our leaders, then, are most likely to be the people we're closest to and know most intimately. We're just more likely to trust people we know, to work harder for people we know, to do our best for people we know, to commit to people we know, and to follow people we know.

You Matter

Something else is revealed by the studies we've cited and the many more that support them. They tell us that you matter and that your leadership matters.

Whatever your role in life may be, you make a difference. There is a 100 percent chance that you can be a role model for leadership. There is a 100 percent chance that you can influence someone else's performance.

There is a 100 percent chance that you can affect what someone else thinks, says, and does. There is a 100 percent chance that you will make a difference in other people's lives.

At this point many people make a comment that goes something like this: "Well, I really believe in this leadership stuff, but, you know, my boss doesn't practice the kind of leadership you're talking about. What am I supposed to do?" Our answer: you can't pass the leadership buck. Just because your manager doesn't do leadership well doesn't excuse you from doing your very best. Your direct reports don't really care about what your manager does, but they care a lot about what you do.

Sure, it'd be really nice if all our leaders were exemplary. It'll be really great if every immediate manager was the gold medal winner in leading—the person everyone looked to as the example of how to be the best leader a person can be. It'd make all our jobs a lot easier, and it'd make us more likely to succeed. The problem is, not all managers are. And even if your manager were the best there is, you still wouldn't be able to relax and say, "Because my manager does this so well, I won't have to worry about how well I perform."

There's no escape. When it comes to leading, you have to take responsibility for the quality of leadership your constituents get. For parents it might be in how you model respect when interacting with your neighbors; for teachers it might be in how you inspire young people to learn; for coaches it might be in how you challenge your players to realize their full potential even when they don't see it; for community leaders it might be in how you enable and encourage citizen participation. You—and that means all of us—are accountable for the leadership you demonstrate.

The question for each of us, then, is not Do I matter? but *How* do I matter? If others look to you for leadership, how are you doing in leading them right now? Not how is my boss doing, or how is the CEO doing, or how is that famous leader doing, but how am *I* doing? None of us needs a ton of statistical studies to tell us how we respond when people are providing terrific leadership and when they're doing a lousy job of it. We just know. When you take an honest look at how you're doing, what's your assessment?

To realize that we make a difference is both a joyous opportunity and a potential burden. Because we most influence those who are the closest to us, we're given a great gift. We're presented with the chance to change a life. We're granted the option of investing in the growth of others. We're offered the opportunity to make the world a better place.

But because we influence most those who are closest to us, we may feel weighed down by the responsibility. We may experience a lot of worry and regret. We may wonder if we're up to the task. We may say to ourselves, "Well, then, I'd better not screw it up."

Don't worry. We humans are amazingly resilient. We can recover from a few losses. We can return from a few setbacks. We can take the bad news. What we can't stand is phoniness and pretension. What we won't suffer are the artificialities of leaders who are only making believe. What we don't respect is a poser. What we don't like is indecisiveness and game playing.

Since *you* are the most important leader in your organization, the only solution to this conundrum is to act. Those who sit around and wait don't leave lasting legacies. Those who stand up and make something happen do.

CHAPTER 5 | No One Likes to Be an Assumption

No one likes being taken for granted. No one likes being ignored, overlooked, or dismissed. Friends don't like it. Spouses don't like it. Children don't like it. Parents don't like it. Employees don't like it.

Saying "Well, I just assumed you knew how much I appreciate what you do" is not going to motivate anyone to higher levels of performance. We all want to know that we're appreciated, and we want to hear it firsthand. How else do we know that we're important to others? How else do we know that others care about us? How else do we know that we matter? Not expressing appreciation to others is equivalent to making them invisible.

Research makes it clear that if we're going to make it to the summit we *need* someone shouting in our ear,

"Come on, you can do it. I know you can do it!" It's not something we easily admit—a lot of times we think we can do it alone. To some, praise and recognition may seem unimportant, inappropriate, or even trivial. But we humans really do need encouragement. Only 2 percent of managers find that encouragement doesn't matter much to them. The rest of us acknowledge that encouragement boosts performance, strengthens our resolve, and improves our health. Otherwise, why perform for an audience? Why not just sing to an empty room, play to an empty arena, or sell to yourself? We need applause to do our best.

Kinko's CEO Gary Kusin learned about the importance of giving recognition the hard way. His 360-degree feedback revealed that he was nearly off the chart—in the *unfavorable* direction—on this dimension, despite being favorably reviewed along most others.

While Gary was generally good at giving recognition at front-line levels in the company, he found out that he wasn't very good at doing it with those in the managerial and executive ranks. Sharing his 360-degree feedback results with his senior team revealed that while they both liked and respected him, and felt he treated them with respect, they pointed out "work is about more than that. Work is about letting people know they're important, their hard work and efforts matter, and they're doing a good job."[1]

It hadn't really occurred to him that senior people wanted or even needed recognition, but as he reflected on it, Gary now says that he realized, "I was wrong." Acting on the insight from his feedback, at one of the weekly staff meetings Gary spotlighted each person on his executive team one at a time and talked about the impact that each person was having on the company. "At first they would blush," he recalled, but then they "sat up proudly because we had done an extraordinary job. We all knew it; we just hadn't talked about it. It was a very emotional time for everyone in the room. It had become obvious that saying 'Thank you, great job. I appreciate you and what you're doing for the company' is the most important thing a leader can do."

Too often leaders assume that *they* don't need encouragement. Maybe other people need it, but they certainly don't. They are, after all, self-motivated professionals, top performers, and accomplished adults. "I'm quite capable of doing fine without it, thank you very much." But they couldn't be more wrong. Says Gary: "I'm one of eight people on the strategic management committee of the corporation, and when my colleagues do something that's really good, I'm getting increasingly comfortable saying so. You know what? They like it. And I have to admit that even though I didn't think I needed positive feedback from them, when I get it, I like it, too."

Maurice Settles, senior station manager with FedEx, confirms that what Gary has to say applies equally to the middle ranks of organizations. One of his managers was convinced that employees really didn't need their supervisor to tell them that they'd done a good job. She thought that their pay and benefits should be recognition enough. Maurice knew otherwise, and found a way to convince her that encouraging others would energize performance. He knew she loved football, so he asked her, "When you go to a football game, do you cheer when the team makes a first down?" She said, "Yes." "What about when the quarterback completes a pass?" he asked. Again the answer was "Yes." Then Maurice made his point. "Why do you do it? Think about it. They get paid to do that. When they score a touchdown, they get paid. We cheer them on anyway, and that's the same thing we should do with our employees." She quickly got the message and immediately started providing more praise and recognition, realizing that people, no matter how much they get paid, still love to hear the roar of approval for a job well done.

You don't have to have a title—CEO or otherwise—to say thank you. Individual contributors are also realizing the importance of appreciation and encouragement. Eric Normington, director of sales at Wide Area Management Services, found opportunities to praise members in the sales and engineering organizations who needed to work together to best serve customer needs. The more he was able to publicly share appreciation for people's support, regardless of which function they represented, the greater, he said, "was the creation of a win-win environment and we further strengthened the bonds between the two groups." Eric shared this insight: "I should not take 'Job Well Dones' for granted even if those people do not report directly to me. You need to take the time to encourage the heart of others because after all everyone appreciates praise, and, at the very least, a thank you."

There are lots of ways to do this, and finding a way to say thank you lets others know that you appreciate the contributions they're making. Not saying thank you can make them feel like what they're doing doesn't matter and that no one really cares. It's similar to the sense we get when we give a gift to someone and then that person never says thanks. It makes us wonder if we should have even bothered. While it may seem ridiculous to think of an extraordinary effort as a gift, especially when people are getting paid, it's a very useful way to frame it. Keep in mind that going above and beyond what is required *is* a choice, and people are more likely to give when their efforts are appreciated.

There are few if any needs more basic than to be noticed, recognized, and appreciated for our efforts. That's as true for volunteers, teachers, doctors, priests, and politicians as it is for the maintenance staff, the sales force, or those in the executive suite. There's little wonder, then, that a greater volume of thanks is reported in highly innovative companies than in less innovative ones. Extraordinary achievements never bloom in barren and unappreciative settings.

Notes of thanks, stickers of approval, or plaques of recognition, however, aren't what earn increased commitment. What makes these gestures effective is our genuine concern and respect for those who are doing the work. We need to accept and acknowledge that nothing really significant can ever be achieved unless people feel appreciated by their leaders. People who are ignored aren't going to put forth the effort it takes to sustain greatness.

There are very few things in life that we can claim to have accomplished without the help of others. In leadership, nothing that we achieve is singular. Nothing. It doesn't matter whether you're the CEO or the shift supervisor, the executive director or the volunteer coordinator, the principal or the team captain; you never, ever do it alone. A leader's legacy is really the legacy of many. Leaders make unique contributions, but others play significant parts. Showing appreciation ensures that everyone will realize that they aren't being taken for granted, that they aren't an assumption, and that they aren't ignored. They will know how important they are to the creation of something meaningful.

PART TWO

Relationships

eadership is a relationship. It's a relationship between those who aspire to lead and those who choose to follow. Whether the relationship is with one or many, leadership requires engaging others. No matter how much formal power and authority our positions give us, we'll only leave a lasting legacy if others *want to* be in that relationship with us. Other people decide whether to follow or run away. Others decide whether to cheer or jeer. Others decide whether to remember us or forget us. No discussion of leadership is complete without considering the quality of the leader-constituent relationship. Leadership requires a resonant connection with others over matters of the heart.

Lasting success depends upon whether we *like* our leaders. It's only logical then that all leaders *should* want to be liked. Not *caring* whether or not you're liked will never bring about the best results. Being motivated to be liked will result in more enabling actions, and these enabling actions—actions such as listening, coaching, developing skills, providing choice, making connections—will create higher levels of performance.

But wanting to be liked does not mean "going along to get along." Exemplary leadership is certainly not a matter of coddling weaknesses or indulging questionable tastes. People don't always see eye to eye, and people don't all have the same personality. Leaders have to learn to be flexible with style but firm on standards, especially in a world rich in diversity. The requirement is to assemble a team of individuals who can vigorously express their differences while also energetically moving in unison toward an ennobling future.

Leading requires trust. It's a prerequisite to getting anything done. And the biggest trust of all is leaving our legacy in the hands of those who come after us. But we can't take trust for granted. We can't just assume it'll always be there when we most need it. We have to constantly work at building it, nurturing it, and sustaining it.

Human history tells us something extremely important about human relationships. It tells us that *people want to be free.* People want to decide things for themselves. People want to shape their own destiny. People want to be in charge of their own lives. The most enduring leadership legacies are those of leaders who have set their people free.

CHAPTER 6 | Leadership Is Personal

During the last couple of years we've had the opportunity to co-facilitate leadership development programs with Ron Sugar, chairman, CEO, and president of Northrop Grumman Corporation. In every one of these sessions, before he ever uttered a word, Ron would walk to the front of the room, sit down at a piano, and play for a few minutes.

After he'd played his last note, Ron would turn to his senior executive colleagues and ask, "Does anyone know why I began this session with playing the piano?" The point, he'd go on to explain, was that if people are going to follow you they need to know more about you than the fact that you're their boss. They need to know something about who you are as a person—your hopes, dreams, talents, expectations, and loves.

"Leadership is personal," Ron would proclaim. He wanted to make clear that "unless *you* know who you are, what you are prepared to do and why" then you can't hope to achieve anything very grand. "Do the people who work for and with you know if you can play the piano?" Ron would ask his colleagues. "Do they know who you are, what you care about, and why they ought to be following you?"

We were sharing this story one day with a group of people from a number of different organizations, and one participant—we'll call him Mike—said he could underscore just how important this point was by telling his own story about his new CEO. It seems this new chief executive was making the rounds in Mike's company, talking about his vision for the firm and how people needed to execute on it. "The CEO was there," Mike explained, "supposedly so people could get to know him. So imagine how flabbergasted everyone was when someone asked him, 'What do you like to do when you are not working?' and he replied rather curtly, 'that's a personal matter and not relevant; next question.'"

"But, that's the point, isn't it!" Mike exclaimed excitedly. "Who is this guy? What does he really care about? Why should we follow—believe and trust—him if we don't know who he is? And he won't tell us!" We could sense Mike's exasperation. We're all just more reluctant to follow people if they're unwilling to tell us about themselves. We start to become a little suspicious. We're less willing to trust.

Ron and Mike are right. People want to know about *you*. They want to know about your values and beliefs, your aims and aspirations, and your hopes and dreams. They want to know who most influenced you, what prepares you for the job you're doing, and what you're like as a person. They want to know what drives you, what makes you happy, and what ticks you off. They want to know if you play the piano—or something else—and they want to know something about your family. This isn't about prying. This is about learning to trust. We're just more likely to trust people we know, and the more we know about our leaders the more likely we are to trust them as human beings. Of course, before you can share any of this with others, you have to have clarity about it yourself. You have to know yourself before others can truly know you.

We've said this many times, and it's worth repeating again. *Leadership is a relationship between those who aspire to lead and those who choose to follow.* There may have been a time when leaders could command commitment, but those times are long past. People follow people, not positions. If there's not some sense of personal relationship, then it's just less likely that people will want to follow.

Ram Dass, the former Harvard professor who became a spiritual teacher, once remarked, "What one person has to offer another is their own being, nothing more and nothing less." The same thing can be said for leaders. *You* are what you offer your constituents. You're not just a brain on legs. You're a whole person full of idiosyncrasies, habits, strengths, weaknesses, successes, failures, loves, hates, and all the other human traits that make up your unique character. To the extent that you withhold any of this from your constituents you deprive them of some of your potential to move them.

Many people believe that leaders shouldn't get too close to their constituents. There's this sense that getting too close to others will not only cloud judgment, it will interfere with the ability to make tough or unpopular decisions that will affect those they're close to. Sergey Nikiforov, co-founder and vice president of product development at Stack3, Inc., told us that he "blindly followed this sort of advice for a few years without giving it too much thought." One day, however, he decided to find out what it would be like to have "normal, human contact" with people in his workplace:

> I made an announcement to my technical staff that I would like to have dinner together at a local restaurant if their schedule permitted it. I got a few strange looks back, and a few rather noncommittal responses. I came to the restaurant a little earlier, and waited at an empty table with anticipation. Would anybody come at all? Would they be suspicious of why we were getting together in such an informal atmosphere, outside of our traditional offices? Eventually, one by one, my colleagues started to arrive.

We sat there in awkward silence, staring at our menus
for a few minutes, until I finally decided to come clean.
I told them there was no specific job-related reason
why we were getting together. All I wanted to do was
to break down those boss-subordinate barriers, and get
to know them better. I knew them as specialists very
well, but I had only a faint idea of who these people
were outside of work. I did not know much about them.
I apologized, and explained that I hoped they would
treat this dinner as a sign of goodwill, as a hand ex-
tended forward to welcome them as individuals, and
not as technical minds.

It turns out they had similar thoughts about me as
well. My subordinates knew me as a boss, and a spe-
cialist, but were rather uncertain about what kind of
person I was outside of the company. We talked for
four straight hours that evening! They were eager to
share about their personal lives, aspirations, hobbies,
vacation plans, and a thousand other things. As I listened to them through the night, I realized how handi-
capped I was before without being connected with my
colleagues at a personal level; how limiting my messages must have been without the benefit of a personal
contact. It turns out that such a simple thing as hanging out at a restaurant could help us find common
ground, and enable us to listen to each other much
more diligently and with open hearts.

We only wish that all leaders could experience
what Sergey did. His revelation is stunning in its honesty

and exposes an essential truth about being the best leader you can be. To be the best you must reveal your humanity. It's the only pathway to a genuine connection with others.

We don't lead our lives in solitary confinement. We lead our lives out in the open. We lead our lives in the company of others, and that is where we leave our legacy. It's the quality of our relationships that most determines whether our legacy will be ephemeral or lasting.

CHAPTER 7 | Leaders *Should* Want to Be Liked

Several years back we invited Irwin Federman to speak to a group of MBA students at Santa Clara University. Irwin, educated in finance, is a former high-technology CEO and now a partner at US Venture Partners. We've interviewed Irwin for a couple of our books, and we felt he had some important insights to share. Irwin said something that day that still makes the hair stand up on the backs of our necks.

"You don't love someone because of who they are," he said, "you love them because of the way they make you feel. This axiom applies equally in a company setting." Many students looked a little bewildered by these comments. The word *love* coming from the mouth of a CEO and venture capitalist must have come as quite a surprise. It wasn't a phrase they were likely to have heard in their companies or their classrooms. Indeed, Irwin acknowledged how unusual it was. "It may seem inappropriate to use words such as *love* and *affection* in relation to business. Conventional wisdom has it that management is not a popularity contest," he said.

Then he hit them with this: "I contend, however, that all other things being equal we will work harder and more effectively for people we like. And we will like them in direct proportion to how they make us feel."

Irwin has it exactly right. We don't need to read mountains of studies on emotional intelligence to understand the truth of his words. *We will work harder and more effectively for people we like. And we will like them in direct proportion to how they make us feel.*

Still, not a week goes by that we don't hear someone in an executive role say something to this effect: "I don't care if people like me. I just want them to respect me." *Get real!* This statement is utter nonsense—contrary to everything we know about effective leadership. Think about it for a moment. Is this a binary choice? Are we restricted to either liking *or* respecting someone? Can't we have both? Can't we both like *and* respect a person?

When we talk to people about the leaders they admire—the ones they'd stay up late for, the ones they'd bust their butts for, the ones they'd die for—we never, ever hear anyone tell us, "Well I hated that woman, but I'd follow her to the ends of the earth!" Or, "He was a real jerk, but I sure was inspired to do my best for him."

The leaders people *want to* follow are the ones for whom they have genuine affection. Love is definitely not too strong a word to use for how the best leaders feel about their constituents and how their constituents feel about these leaders.

If we absolutely can't have both liking and respect, then we'll choose liking over respect. While people may have to defer to the sheer power and brute force of a bully, none of us want to be in the same room with a bully unless we have to. We want to get as far away as possible. When we don't like someone we don't want to be around that person, we don't want to work for that person, we don't want to perform for that person, and we don't want to do business with that person.

Our research, and practically everyone else's on the subject, clearly shows that people perform significantly more effectively when their leaders treat them with dignity and respect, listen to them, support them, recognize them, make them feel important, build their skills, and show confidence in them. Likability is a major factor in being successful in just about every endeavor in life.

Being liked will also make your job as a leader a whole lot easier. You'll have an easier time getting people to trust you. You'll have an easier time getting people to listen to you. You'll have an easier time getting people to put in extra effort. You'll have an easier time getting people to accept bad news. You'll have an easier time getting people to work together. You'll have an easier time making money. And you'll also be a much healthier person.

So when someone says, "I don't care if people don't like me," can they really be serious? We don't think so. How can anyone mean it when the evidence is so clear and compelling that being liked produces better results? And, who are the "people" they are talking about, anyway? Can they really mean that they don't care if their spouses don't like them, or their kids don't like them, or their business partners don't like them, or their employees don't like them, or their friends (would they have any?) don't like them?

When we dig below the shallow surface of this comment, what is it that these people are trying to say? Perhaps it's this: "If I get close enough to people for them to like me, then I'll have a tough time doing the difficult parts of my job. Things like firing people, reprimanding them for poor performance, or holding them accountable for living up to high standards. This will be really hard for me, and so to do it I have to put on a suit of armor so I won't get hurt or feel bad about the tough things I have to do."

For most of us, these feelings are probably closer to the truth than "I don't care if they like me." We all enjoy more the inspirational, energizing, innovative, upbeat parts of our work. We don't relish the tasks that may adversely affect others or make us feel guilty or cause sleepless nights. When it comes to leading others, it'd be terrific if we only had to do the things that brought great joy to people's lives and to our own.

A tough truth about leading—and one that doesn't get talked about enough—is that sometimes you hurt others and sometimes you get hurt. You can't hit the delete key and eliminate these times from your job. You can't delegate them to others. They come with the territory.

It's also true that when you're in a leadership role, the chances are great that *not everyone is going to like you.* When you take a strong stand on guiding values and on a vision of the future, there's no way that everyone is going to be happy about what you say and what you do.

This truth, however, should not deter us from *wanting* to be liked. Being motivated to have others like us will result in more empowering actions on our part than just wanting to be respected. Being motivated to want others to like us will make us more concerned about them than we are about ourselves.

When sharing these thoughts at a conference recently, we added a corollary observation: "If people don't want to be liked then they probably don't belong in leadership." Sharon Jordan-Evans, executive coach and coauthor of *Love 'em or Lose 'em,* thought our observation should be modified slightly. She thought we should add, "Unless the person is motivated to change their behavior." She told us about an individual she was coaching. This particular executive was troubled by some feedback he'd gotten. "People tell me I'm the smartest guy around," he related to her. Sharon was curious as to why this feedback troubled him. He said, "I still want to be thought of as smart; I also want to be thought of as the nicest guy around." There's hope for this leader. Nice *and* smart, friendly *and* tough, loving *and* demanding are not polar opposites in real life. In real life this makes us human.

Of course, you have to work hard at being liked. It's not just about your winning personality. It's about how you act when you're around others. It's about your behavior. And if it's a behavior, there's a skill involved. And if there's a skill involved, you can learn to perform it better than you now do *if* you want to. As Irwin said, "people will like us in direct proportion to how we make them feel." It takes a lot of effort to make people feel encouraged, confident, cared for, and capable of doing more than even they thought possible.

And here's a final piece of advice. If you have people working for you in leadership roles who truly don't care if other people don't like them, then fire them. *They* may not like you, but everyone else will.

CHAPTER 8

When You Don't See Eye to Eye, Seek to Understand

How can you lead others when you don't see eye to eye with the leader you're supposed to follow? It can be frustrating beyond words when your leader doesn't share your values, your vision, or your passion for the same things. It can challenge you to your core. It can test your dedication. It can keep you awake at night. It can make you question your own judgment. It can make others wonder if you're weak. It can raise questions about your credibility. It can diminish your sense of self-worth. It can put your own legacy at risk.

Our gut instincts may tell us to quit. Get out. Flee. It's a natural inclination that has served our species well since the time of the saber-toothed tiger. The question is, Where do we go? We'll never agree with everything our leaders do, and we'll frequently have to deal with many people—direct reports, colleagues, customers, friends, and family—with whom we don't agree and who don't agree with us. Fleeing is really not a viable option. Besides, it's tough to leave a legacy if you leave the relationship.

Sometimes fleeing is a recommended option, of course. If you work for someone who is dishonest, manipulative, or unethical, blow the whistle and get out of there. Your courage in exposing fraud, deception, malfeasance, harassment, and prejudice may serve as an example to others. But these are not the norm. More often than not, things are not that clear-cut.

Consider the lesson that Eric Piziali, senior financial analyst at Hitachi Data Systems, told us he learned when he decided to stick around and find ways to exert his leadership despite disagreements.

> Early in my career finding another job would have sounded like solid advice as well as a probable solution. However, as I think back on the past ten years in the corporate work environment, I realize now that this is also an opportunity to develop skills that will help in a multitude of future encounters. Specifically, it is an opportunity to show your leadership skills and find ways to work with people you don't always agree with. I think people notice when you are having difficulty working with someone, but they also notice when you find ways to make it work. In other words, you begin to shine as someone who can be trusted and is capable of leadership.

Experience is a great teacher, and not all experiences are going to be pleasant. Many will be filled with conflict and tension. Working with people with whom you have difficulty is a terrific laboratory. It can help you learn how to handle the most challenging circumstances.

Our colleague, consultant and author Roger Harrison, once said to us after a particularly difficult encounter, "Your enemy is your teacher." At first, we thought Roger was nuts. Maybe he'd attended one too many sensitivity training sessions and read one too many New Age books. But the more we reflected on what he had to say, the more sense it made. What Roger was telling us was that in every serious conflict there's something about ourselves we have the chance to learn. Whenever you find yourself in a serious conflict with someone, ask yourself, "What is it that I need to learn? What is this person or situation trying to teach me?" You may find out what's really important to you. You may become conscious about a deficiency in your own abilities. You may realize what's at stake for you. What's crucial is that you become more self-aware—and self-awareness is a predictor of success in leadership.

The Only Person You Can Change Is You

Learning more about ourselves is the first step toward overcoming differences. Learning more about others is the second. Consider how Elaine Mathews, a market analyst at LSI Logic, learned this lesson.

> Two years ago my current boss became my boss, and she really did not think highly of my work. This was frustrating because I had always been a motivated worker who had been recognized as a star performer by our senior executives, but she was not familiar with my line of work. So I decided to talk to her about how she measured "good work," and we came up with projects together that we discussed weekly and reflected on quarterly. While I had always been used to a formal, professional communication style, I noticed that she liked to communicate in a very casual, almost friend-to-friend manner, so I tried to adjust my speech to be in sync with hers.
>
> Over time as we walked through projects together, she learned that I was very dedicated to quality work and that I was someone she could depend on and trust. I explained to her how I wanted to get into strategic planning and eventually she supported me to pursue a special project in that department—which went very well. I was relieved to find that my first review was fairly positive, and my second review was almost outstanding.

By engaging with her manager, Elaine learned something valuable about the other person. She also learned that she could adapt. She learned that she could change the way she communicated and as a result change the perception her manager had of her.

Many disagreements aren't a matter of right or wrong. The world is too complex for that. Maybe it's your approach to dealing with someone else that's not working. The wisest advice we can give is never to expect someone else to change. You have no control over that. The only person you control is yourself, and sometimes even that is in doubt!

We need to take the responsibility to reach out and engage, creating a communication channel that works for both parties and letting our managers know how they can help us succeed. Understanding our managers' working styles and being sensitive to their challenges can also go a long way toward creating an effective working partnership. Even in the best of partnerships, disagreements and conflicts will arise. Being able to relate the conflict to specific issues and to keep from taking it personally is essential.

Focus on the Purpose and Not the Person

When we actively engage with others in difficult conversations, we frequently learn that while there are serious differences in style, we may actually be aligned on our goals and objectives. We can find ourselves in agreement

with the same ends as others, even while we find ourselves in disagreement about the possible paths to that
future. If we learn that our hearts may be in the same
place, it'll be a lot easier to move forward.

This principle applies to all relationships—to our
leaders, to our colleagues, and to our direct reports. Amy
Goldfine recalled the importance of this when she told
us about being general manager of WTUL, Tulane University's student-run radio station. WTUL had over a hundred
DJs and an executive staff of about thirty, and she had a
particularly difficult time working with one woman on
the executive staff.

> [Karyn] had a very negative attitude and poor interper-
> sonal communication skills, and was rather disrespect-
> ful to me on a number of occasions. However, she was
> a hard worker and put in a lot of time on a job that
> nobody else wanted to do, so she was continually re-
> appointed to her position.
>
> After one particularly frustrating encounter, I was
> sitting in my adviser's office complaining about this
> woman, and my adviser said to me, "Amy, you're never
> going to change Karyn. But just remember, her heart is
> in the right place. She loves this station as much as
> you." And she was right. Karyn was dedicated to the
> same cause I was. I can't say that I was *never* bothered
> by her again, but I found myself able to ignore a lot of
> her difficult attributes because we were striving for the
> same goal.

When you're in a difficult and tense situation, the first and most important thing to find out is if everyone involved shares the same purpose and goals. It's crucial to talk about desired outcomes and make every effort to get everyone aligned. Once you're working toward the same set of goals and operating by the same set of norms, you'll be less likely to second-guess each other's motives and more likely to understand, and be less bothered by, each other's working styles.

Promote Constructive Insubordination

We'd even go a bit further. Leaders have to be able to promote, demonstrate, and support *constructive insubordination*. It's been said that "if both of us are always agreeing, then one of us is redundant," and this is no more true than today. When everyone agrees, especially just for the sake of getting along, we're unlikely to achieve the best outcomes. To test this notion researchers asked fifty groups of students to solve a murder mystery. They found that groups of people who had the most diverse social backgrounds and experiences were the most likely to solve the case. Not only were homogeneous groups more likely to be wrong, they were also more likely to express greater confidence in their answers despite being wrong!

We can't afford to surround ourselves with yes-people. We need to have people willing to support us and also willing to voice their disagreements. Others will see issues that we don't see—perhaps never even thought about—and may even come up with a better solution than our own.

Historian Doris Kearns Goodwin tells the story of how Abraham Lincoln consciously and willfully assembled a cabinet made up the very men he had defeated in the election. Kearns called them a "team of rivals." She says this of Lincoln's skill:

> This, then, is a story of Lincoln's political genius revealed through his extraordinary array of personal qualities that enabled him to form friendships with men who had previously opposed him; to repair injured feelings that, left untended, might have escalated into permanent hostility; to assume responsibility for the failures of subordinates; to share credit with ease; and to learn from mistakes.[1]

We all could take a lesson from Abraham Lincoln. If he could manage to lead a team of rivals under the extraordinary challenges of the Civil War, we could certainly find it within ourselves to manage the conflicts we face, modest as they are by comparison to his.

We have to make it possible for people to argue with each other—up, down, in, out, and sideways—if we are to realize the best from today's diverse and talented workforce. We shouldn't strive to win every skirmish, but instead endeavor to unite in our decisions so that we can win the battles that matter most. The legacy that comes from difficult conversations will be far more creative and sustaining than ones that come from people who always see eye to eye.

CHAPTER 9

You Can't Take Trust for Granted

rust is the social glue that binds human relationships. Without it we'd be unable to get anything meaningful accomplished. But sometimes our trust is tested. Ours certainly was a short while back.

In one of the frequent leadership workshops we conduct, Barry was facilitating an activity called the "trust fall." You may have done this yourself, but in case you haven't, imagine the following scenario.

Your work group is at an off-site meeting, participating in some team-building exercises, one of which is the trust fall. Team members stand in two rows of six people each, about two feet apart, and face one another. At the head of the rows is a stepladder. Each team member is invited to step onto the top of the four-foot ladder, turn to face away from the group, cross both arms, remain straight and stiff, and then fall over backwards. The team's common goal is to catch each person by putting up their arms at exactly the same time, making a safe cradle for each falling colleague.

The first person climbs the ladder, and on cue falls backward. Every member of the team reaches out and catches the person. They lower her safely to the ground. The faller heaves a sigh of relief and thanks everyone for doing their jobs. The second person now goes up to the top of the ladder. On cue, he falls over backward and is caught. And this continues for everyone in the group, with the team adjusting as needed each time depending upon the demands of the situation. (Is the faller heavy or light? Is the faller tall or short?)

The people are feeling pretty good about themselves and their ability to work together. They've seen firsthand how trust works, what it means to put their trust in others, and what it means to know that someone else trusts them. You and your teammates get to experience how trust connects each to all the rest, and how by working together they can do something that none of them can do by themselves.

Both of us have seen and participated in this team-building exercise hundreds of times over the years. On one occasion recently the group had a few extra minutes before needing to start the next activity, so they asked

Barry if he'd be willing to be the faller. Here's what pro-
ceeded to happen as Barry experienced it:

> Since I'd done this many times before I suggested a
> new variation. I said to the group, "How about if I get
> on the ground, in the same path as the person falling,
> and take a photograph of everyone catching one of
> you as he falls? So, remember, you have to catch this
> person, like you've done before, because if you don't
> they will fall right on top of me!" I added, "Having
> observed you do this for one another, I trust you can
> do this again."
>
> So the team gets itself organized to do what it has
> just done successfully ten times in a row without fail-
> ure. But this time around it seems that a few members
> of the team aren't paying attention to the task at hand,
> and they don't put their arms up at the same time as
> everyone else does. The remaining group members
> can't bear the faller's weight and don't catch the faller.
> He tumbles through their arms and right on top of me.
> The faller's not injured—after all he had something
> soft to fall on!—but I get the wind knocked out of me.
> (I will subsequently be diagnosed with several cracked
> ribs.)
>
> The various group members help me get back on
> my feet. They exclaim: "Sorry." "Are you all right?"
> "Are you sure you are all right?" "Does anything hurt?"
> "I guess we really screwed up, right?" "We didn't pay
> enough attention." "We were too cocky." "Suppose
> you'll never do this again, will you?"

I take a few moments to catch my breath. I think about how to respond to all of these various concerns and comments, but especially the last one, "Suppose you'll never do this again, will you?" which is code for "You trusted us and now look what happened."

What's the lesson? There's a sucker born every minute, and this time it was me? After a few minutes of catching my breath and considering the options, I thought I saw two key rules emerge from this experience (although I'm not recommending this particular piece of experiential learning for anyone):

Rule #1: You have to keep working on trust and never take it for granted. Of course, this is true for all relationships.

Rule #2: Sometimes trust breaks down. So, see Rule #1.

I still live by these rules, including taking part in Trust Falls when it feels right for the group. The occasion didn't arise again that day, as we moved on to other exercises, but the breakdown seemed to do more to cement the learning about trust than all the successes did.

You Can't Take Trust for Granted

What does trust look like? Trust is openness. Trust is valuing other people such that you respect their opinions and perspectives. You listen to them. Trust means moving outside your comfort zone and letting go of always doing it your way, or even the way that "it's always been done before." Trust requires honesty with oneself as well as with others. Trust means not making commitments you can't keep; it requires not overpromising no matter how much you wish you could do something. Trust requires a willingness to let others take charge, and to let others, at times, make mistakes in doing things they have never done before.

For leaders, trust is the willingness to be vulnerable and open up to others even when doing so may risk real harm. (Like people falling on top of you!) Trust is relying on others, having confidence in others, and this can be difficult for the best of us, but especially for leaders. If trusting means making yourself vulnerable and you're the leader, then that means your life and career are on the line, too. You're exposed to the consequences of their actions, not just to your own. Leaders don't like to feel defenseless, weak, helpless, and at risk. This is the antithesis of the impervious, invincible, indomitable image of the leader that is created in the press and portrayed in comic books. It's the opposite of Donald Trump on *The Apprentice* bellowing, "You're fired!"

But if you don't trust, then what? Many things just won't get done. You're left with doing more and more work yourself. You're left with constantly checking up on other people's work, spending time micromanaging. You're left with getting less than the best from your team. And the more you don't trust them—the less faith and confidence you express and demonstrate in them—the less they come to trust you in return. Eventually, you burn out from the workload and stress. Indeed, one of the top impediments to career success is the inability to trust others.

So, if you want the best relationships and outcomes, you have to trust. And you have to understand that in the game of trust, it's leaders who have to ante up first. This means taking a lot of time to build relationships. It means listening carefully to others. It means getting to know about their capabilities, needs, and aspirations. It means talking about values and being clear about norms—for example, what's acceptable or unacceptable in terms of how people treat each other, regardless of their place in the organization. It means being on the same page about performance standards, customer expectations, and about *why* what we do matters.

Sometimes Trust Breaks Down

Sometimes, despite our best efforts (and theirs), people don't do their jobs. Sometimes they let us down. Sometimes they betray us. Sometimes the social bond of trust comes unglued. What do we do?

The temptation may be to hold on tighter. You don't volunteer. You want to play it safe. You want to hide and not expose yourself to risk. But what happens then? What happens when you constantly look over other people's shoulders and check up on other people's work? What happens when you send them signals that you don't trust them? Naturally, they begin not to trust you. It becomes a vicious cycle. When we as leaders succumb to this temptation, we end up building barriers. We end up looking out for our own interests and not for the interests of the organization. We end up with lower levels of performance. You may think you're preserving your position this way, but you're not. Eventually people will leave the relationship with you—unless, of course, you're asked to leave first.

Your only option is to see rule number one. Keep working on building and sustaining trust. Keep working on the relationships, on the common understandings. What happened that day when the team let one of their members drop through their arms happened precisely because everyone took trust for granted! They assumed that everyone was doing what they were capable of doing, and would continue to do so, but for that one moment they didn't.

The neat thing is that because the team learned from that particular moment that taking trust for granted can have some negative consequences, you should have seen their performance for the rest of the day. They continually checked in with and looked out for one another.

And because they fully appreciated how their leader didn't give up on them and didn't lose faith in them even when they goofed up, they worked more diligently and productivity than anyone might have imagined. That's the real legacy from trust.

CHAPTER 10

Let Your People Go

"an you provide leadership development for this organization?" a division manager asked us. Then without taking a breath he wondered aloud, "But what worries me about this idea is that if they were all leaders then how would I get them to work together?" Developing leaders throughout an organization can be a very scary thought, especially for those in hierarchical settings. If everyone's acting like a leader with the freedom to change the business-as-usual environment, then it seems like there'll just be mass chaos. *Freedom,* for some, conjures up visions of anarchy. But the opposite is actually the case. The more you control others, the more likely it is that they will rebel. Exemplary leaders have repeatedly told us that they get the greatest commitment precisely when they let their people go.

Consider Samta Bansal's experience in turning around her team at the multinational corporation where she works: "What worked best for me was the freedom and power I gave to my team; the trust and confidence I showed in them. It increased their commitment level to the project." She told us how these actions required concerted effort: "The concept of giving away power was not in my comfort zone. But what I learned doing it was a great humbling experience. Once I consciously started to create a climate of trust and started giving independence to my team, the sense of responsibility and accountability increased. People started to own the tasks instead of considering it a team liability." Samta, like other leaders we've worked with, realized that expanding freedom of choice increases personal responsibility, commitment, and productivity.

No One Wants a Micromanager

When we asked Bruce Hillsberg, director of government storage solutions at IBM, how he maintains a high-performing team, without any prompting he replied, "Hire smart and capable people and then let them do what they do best." Bruce lets people know what has to be done and then trusts them to do it. Moreover, like so many of us today, he is way too busy to keep track of what all his employees are doing.

However, Bruce didn't start off with this attitude. In 1998 he was assigned the responsibility of ensuring that all of IBM's internal applications were ready for the year 2000. Bruce had been responsible for leading teams before, but this was his first corporate-wide high-profile leadership assignment—one that was critically important to the company with an unchangeable deadline. Originally he was very concerned about how he would perform. Because of this, he took a rather tight-leashed approach to his employees and their progress. He wanted constant updates and needed to be reassured they were doing their jobs. This went on for a few months, and he was actually thinking he was doing a pretty good job. He was working an insane amount of hours but figured that came with the position. Eventually one of his subordinates, who had worked with Bruce in other capacities, finally had enough and approached him about the problems with his management style.

This thirty-year IBM veteran was much respected in what he did. He sat down with Bruce and made him realize that his employees were more than capable of executing the task given to them. He pointed out to Bruce that he was becoming like a boss whose micromanagement they both had despised in the past. That approach had made both of them feel like anyone could perform their tasks and took away their self-worth.

This was a turning point for Bruce. He sat back and thought about his constituents and realized they were very good at what they did. This realization changed his approach from micromanaging to letting his people go and do what they do best. Over the course of the next few months, the productivity of the team soared, and in the end the transition to Y2K was smooth, with no problems. Bruce was promoted to director as a result.

Some people will always resist accepting more freedom and independence. They may feel unprepared for the responsibility. Certainly, we shouldn't and wouldn't want to inflict independence in cases where people's inexperience could cause them and others real harm. But we won't know what people are capable of if we don't give them the opportunity to grow and develop. One way to make this happen is to provide them with the chance to make choices. Freedom means having a choice.

Give People Freedom of Choice

Motivation has to come from within. Even if people were to do something while we were watching over their shoulders, if they lacked the internal drive to do it—that feeling of personal enthusiasm and interest—their work would come to a screeching halt the moment we stopped monitoring them. The only effective approach to sustaining performance is to tap into people's natural drive for autonomy, and invite people to join in the adventure.

Did you know that if you were sitting at a table with us and predicting the probability of pulling a number out of a hat, you'd predict that you have a much better chance of winning if you know that it's your hand that will do the picking rather than one of ours? The odds are the same, but when you do the picking you *feel* more in control of the outcome. This is precisely the point we all need to understand. If the leaders do the picking, their constituents will feel less confident in the outcomes. If *they* do the picking, they will feel more confident in the outcome. And leaders also need to understand that their own chances of picking "the right number"—that is, making the right decision—are not any better, and probably worse, than if the team makes the decision. Keep in mind that when *Fortune* magazine reviewed recent notable failures of corporate leaders, the culprit wasn't the leaders' vision but the lack of commitment by others in the execution.

It's all about feeling personally responsible for a decision or action. The internal dialogue we go through sounds something like this: "There were alternatives. I wasn't forced. It was my choice. I had a realistic picture of what one alternative would entail over another and I selected this one. There's nobody else to blame, no one other than I who can take responsibility for the success or failure of this decision. So I'd better do what's required to make this work!"

Choice is the glue that binds individuals to actions, motivating them to accept responsibility. How choice leads to commitment is evident from our discussions with hundreds of working professionals about projects they worked on that were successful and others that failed or were less than successful. Over and over again we've learned that the best predictor of a project's failure or success is whether people volunteered or were assigned to it. In volunteering, they indicate their belief that they can do what's required. People who believe they can do something are considerably more likely to be successful than those who don't expect to do well. Choice unleashes people's internal drive—and their leadership—to do what's necessary to make things happen.

Organizational consultant Neale Clapp once told us that he believed the fundamental tension for people in organizations was the tension between freedom and constraint. When do we delegate and when do we decide? When do we rebel against authority and when do we accept it? When do we empower others and when do we use positional power? When do we break the rules and when do we set limits? When do we listen and when do we tell? When do we let go and when do we hold on?

To say that leaders should always increase freedom and relax all constraints is intellectually dishonest and totally unrealistic. To say that constituents should always accept constraints and never challenge the status quo is equally dishonest and unrealistic. We can count on people to strive to be free. We can also count on organizations to exert constraints. Part of our job as leaders is to engage people in grappling with the tension between freedom and constraint.

More freedom is becoming the norm. But it would be foolish and irresponsible to expect organizations to abandon all constraints. Institutions must have limits; the question is not whether there are constraints but how many, how much, and of what type.

Personal Responsibility

The decision to sign on, get out, or rebel is an issue of personal responsibility. Personal responsibility is a hot phrase these days; management specialists, human resource professionals, politicians, and self-help gurus like Dr. Phil tell us we need more of it. But what does it really mean to be *responsible?*

When we looked up *responsibility* in *The Great Ideas: A Syntopicon of Great Books of the Western World,* the index directed us to "punishment, sin, and will."[1] *Punishment. Sin. Will.* From Aeschylus and Sophocles to the Old and New Testaments to Hegel and Kant, the personal responsibility discourse has been about whether people freely choose their actions or whether they are divinely predestined to act in certain ways. Hence "free will." Freely choosing to do something is an indispensable condition for successful execution. Without the belief that free choice leads to more responsible action, all modern organizations would have to centralize power at the top and put a cop on every corner.

Personal responsibility can exist only if people have free will and if they exercise it. Personal responsibility cannot exist independent of choice. In personally choosing to act, individuals are saying explicitly or implicitly, "I will accept the consequences of my actions." Personal credibility hinges on the belief that we human beings are personally accountable for our own actions. People are held accountable against the standard of shared values upon which the members of the group, organization, society, or culture have agreed. Ignoring this precept, as many leaders have in not accepting the consequences of their own actions, contributes to increased cynicism throughout the workforce.

To make a meaningful difference we each have to make our own meaningful choices. If leaders steal from others the opportunities to make such choices, they steal a bit of the legacy those others might have created. People can't make their own mark if someone else is holding their hand all the time. At some point you have to let go of that hand and leave others to write their own histories.

PART THREE

Aspirations

eople commit to causes, not to plans. Commitment is fueled by what we cherish. If the values about which we care deeply are vividly clear to us, then the whims of fashion and the opinion polls won't sidetrack us. A lasting legacy is built on a firm foundation of principles and purpose.

That means that leadership development is first and foremost self-development. Becoming a leader begins with an exploration of the inner territory as we search to find our own authentic voice. Leaders must decide on what matters in life, before they can live a life that matters.

Leaders are expected to look into the future, to gaze across the time horizon and communicate to us what they see. It's not about being prescient or clairvoyant. It's about being discerning and perceptive. It's about noticing what's around the corner.

Yet as much as we want leaders to be forward-looking, they aren't. Being forward-looking may differentiate leaders from other credible people, but it's the skill at which leaders are the most inept. Our future legacies are being taken hostage by our present-centeredness. To leave something meaningful behind we have to devote time to creating something valuable ahead.

Another thing to keep in mind: the future doesn't belong just to the leaders. It's not just the leader's vision that leaders are accountable for enacting. Leadership isn't about selling *your* vision; it's about articulating the people's vision.

We leave a legacy to others. They are our inheritors. If you're going to leave a legacy that means something to others, you have to think about what they want and what they aspire to achieve.

Leadership is also not the private property of a few at the top. Leadership is a common area that's accessible to everyone. The best leaders turn their followers into leaders, realizing that the journey ahead requires many guides. Exemplary leaders also have the confidence to turn themselves into followers, trusting that many others are also eager and competent to make a difference in the world.

CHAPTER 11 | Lead from the Inside Out

Authentic leadership does not come from the outside in. It comes from the inside out. Inside-out leadership means becoming the author of your own story and the maker of your own history.

All serious leadership starts from within. That's the only way we'll ever be able to respond to what our constituents most expect and want from us. And what is that? What they most want from us is that we be genuinely who we are.

Just imagine this scene. Someone walks into the room right now and announces to you and your colleagues, "Hi, I'm your new leader." At that very moment, what do you want to know from this person? What are the questions that immediately pop into your mind?

We've asked this question of many different groups, and the responses are almost always the same. People tell us they want to ask that new leader these questions:

- Who are you?
- What do you stand for and believe in?
- Where do you want to take us?
- Why you?
- What qualifies you for this job?
- What makes you think you can do this?
- Do you really know what you're getting yourself into?
- What changes are you planning to make?

Questions like these get to the heart of leadership. People always want to know something about the person doing the leading before they're going to become the people doing the following. They want to know about the person behind the mask. They want to know what gives us the confidence to think that we can actually pull this off. If we're to leave a lasting legacy—regardless of the scale or scope of our aspirations—then we have to wrestle with questions such as these until we find answers that give meaning to our actions and to our lives.

The quest for leadership, therefore, is first an inner quest to discover who you are, and it's through this process of self-examination that you find the awareness needed to lead. Self-confidence is really awareness of and faith in your own powers, and these powers become clear and strong only as you work to identify and develop them. The mastery of the art of leadership comes with the mastery of the self, and so developing leadership is a process of developing the self.

Leadership Begins When Something Grabs Hold of Us

Developing ourselves as leaders begins with knowing our own key convictions; it begins with our value system. Clarifying our own values and aspirations is a highly personal matter, and no one else can do it for us. To exhibit harmonious leadership—leadership in which our words and deeds are consonant—we must be in tune internally. We must know who we are, what's important to us, and what is not.

When Mike Sullivan started his new position in investor relations at Intel, he knew that he had to find what "grabbed him and wouldn't let go." He told us that he spent a lot of time thinking deeply about his values, talking them over with his spouse and closest friends, and that while this reflection was difficult, even challenging at times, it was well worth the struggle. In turn, he realized that the leadership challenges he was facing at work were the result of "preconceived ideas about leadership that were stereotypical, outdated, and simply wrong."

Exploring his inner territory led Mike to become clear on something that had been a great mystery to him for years. He told us, "I realized that passion inspires me to lead and that I will need to make manifest in my work those things I am passionate about in order to want to lead and to be emotive and empathetic with my constituents." As a result of exploring and then struggling to make choices about what was really important, Mike became conscious of his values, so he felt more grounded and confident. He explained how this insight directly impacted his leadership behavior:

> I'd assumed a new position with responsibility for my company's relationships with the Wall Street brokerage analysts who publish earnings estimates and buy/sell recommendations on our stock. We'd been suffering from Wall Street's perception that a competitor was gaining momentum in the market. Whereas I might ordinarily wait for my boss (who previously drove this function) to devise a response, I felt confident in developing an engagement plan, crafting the story and messages, setting up meetings with analysts, and pulling senior managers into interviews to tell the analysts how we planned to compete and recover lost ground. Identifying my values and finding my voice was what gave me the confidence to take the initiative in my first weeks in a very visible new job.

Leadership begins with something that grabs hold of us and won't let go. And this "something" will only be found when we are willing to take a journey through our inner territory—a journey that often requires opening doors that are shut, walking in dark spaces that are frightening, and touching the flame that burns. But at the end is truth.

Clarity of Values Builds Solid Support

This is precisely what we've found in several of our own studies. Clarity of personal values matters greatly to our feeling motivated, creative, and committed to our workplaces. When we're clear about our personal values we feel empowered, ready and prepared to take action. Ready to be a leader.

Tanveer Ahmad, engineering manager at Sony Corporation of America, echoed these sentiments when he told us what he had learned: "Clarifying one's values and expressing oneself clearly and confidently is an essential first step that leaders must undertake in order to build a firm grounding. There are no shortcuts, work-arounds, or other easy alternatives to this primal step in the leadership journey." Tanveer went on to explain, "One immediate payoff in developing a clear sense of values and communicating these values is that it serves to enlist willing constituents and builds a vital support base for the leader."

We've all heard the expression "Leaders stand up for their beliefs." Tanveer reminds us that to serve as a solid platform on which to stand, our beliefs must be clear to us and clearly communicated to others. When these values are matched by our deeds, we've earned the credibility required for others to put their trust in us, wanting to climb up and join us on that platform, knowing they'll be supported.

When you're not clear about your personal values it's hard to imagine how you can stand up for your beliefs, isn't it? How can you speak out if you don't know what's important to you? How can you have the courage of your convictions if you have no convictions? Leaders who aren't clear about what they believe are likely to change their position with every fad or opinion poll. Without core beliefs and with only shifting positions, would-be leaders are judged as inconsistent and derided for being political in their behavior.

We all know deep down that people can only speak the truth when speaking in their own voice. The techniques and tools that fill the pages of management and leadership books are not substitutes for who and what we are. In fact they can boomerang if thrown by a spin meister who's mastered form but not substance.

After all, who's the very first person you have to lead? Who's the first person that must be willing to follow you? You are, of course. Until you passionately believe in something it's hard to imagine that you could ever convince anyone else to believe. And if you wouldn't follow you, why should anyone else?

Developing leadership capacity is not about stuffing in a whole bunch of new information or trying out the latest technique. It's about leading out of what is already in your soul. It's about liberating the leader within you. It's about setting yourself free. It's about putting your ear to your heart and just listening.

Clarity of values is essential in knowing which way, for each of us, is north, south, east, or west. The clearer we are, the easier it is to stay on the path we've chosen. In exploring our inner territory and finding our voice we calibrate an inner compass by which to navigate the course of our daily lives and to take the first steps along the journey of making a difference.

So—back to that leader who walks in the room and says, "Hi. I'm your new leader." Suppose it's you. How would you answer the questions that others want to know about why they should follow you? What would you say when asked, "Who are you?"

CHAPTER 12

Forward-Looking Is a Leadership Prerequisite

Y ou can leave a lasting legacy only if you can imagine a brighter future, and the capacity to imagine exciting future possibilities is the defining competence of leaders. Today's leaders have to be concerned about tomorrow's world and those who will inherit it. They are the custodians of the future, and it's their job to make sure that they leave their organizations in better shape than they found them.

We've surveyed thousands of people on what they want in their leaders, and they tell us that being *forward-looking* is second only to honesty as their most admired leader quality. On average, 72 percent of respondents select it. In Asia, Europe, and Australia the preference for forward-looking is a full ten percentage points higher than it is in America. At the more senior levels in organizations, those selecting *forward-looking* is nearly 90 percent. This isn't just confirmed in our own studies. Every serious student of the subject asserts that leaders must have the capacity to envision an uplifting and ennobling image of the future and to enlist others in a common purpose.

That's the good news.

Here's the bad news. *Today's leaders stink at it.* While being forward-looking is a highly valued leadership competence, it's the one leaders are least capable of demonstrating. And there's more bad news. Those of us who help leaders become better at creating and communicating visions of the future stink at it, too.

We know this because, ever since we started measuring leadership practices, this is the competency that has shown up as being the least understood, appreciated, and demonstrated. Leaders report that they're not very good at or comfortable with envisioning the future and enlisting others in a common vision. The feedback from their constituents is even more negative. This is the skill set at which the vast majority of leaders need to become significantly more capable.

So here's the question. If there's reliable evidence and general consensus that it's so important for leaders to articulate a vision and get others excited about it, why do leaders do so poorly at it? If academics and practitioners alike agree on its value, why are we still struggling after so many years to develop this capacity in leaders—and what can we do about it?

We're Hostage to the Present

Whenever we ask our clients and students about these low scores, the most frequent explanation is that people and organizations today are hostage to the present. The demands of our business culture, people say, keep us focused on quarterly profits, preventing leaders from spending enough time thinking beyond the next three months. In nonprofits and government agencies, it's the current crisis that consumes the majority of everyone's time.

Another thing that keeps people from thinking for the long term, we're told, is the pace of change. Things are just moving so fast that many believe it's impossible to know what's going to be happening in a year, let alone three, five, or ten years. Then there's the increased complexity of problems. Everything seems to be related to everything else. And there's also all the frightening uncertainty in the world. It's tough to get a clear picture of where you're headed when the landscape keeps shifting. And finally, most leaders feel overworked. How can you squeeze in time to think about the future when you are too tired to think about what you're going to have for dinner?

All these explanations have some truth to them. The workload is unlikely to get much lighter anytime soon. Wall Street does apply constant pressure to meet or exceed investors' quarterly expectations, and punishes organizations if they don't. Citizens want action now on critical issues that affect their lives. Customers want their needs met today. And we only have to look at the headlines to know how rapidly things change and how complex and uncertain our world is. Few, if any, of us anticipated that Paris suburbs would be burning, that flooding from busted levees would devastate the historic city of New Orleans, that pirates would be raiding a cruise ship off the coast of Africa, or that we'd be stockpiling vaccines in case of a global epidemic of bird flu.

How can we possibly be more forward-looking when we're driving under the influence of all these pressures?

Pay More Attention

We're sorry to say it, but none of the pressures that hold you hostage are going to go away. The likelihood is minuscule that investors, citizens, employees, or customers are going to stop insisting that leaders remain vigilant about current operations. New advances in technology will offer daily surprises. International disputes will still threaten our security, and natural disasters will create hardship and heartache. The world will continue to serve up unexpected challenges. That's just the way it is. Even so, people still want leaders to be forward-looking. That won't change either.

Despite the daily pressures that hold our minds hostage, we *can* be more future-oriented. As counterintuitive as it might seem, the best place to start creating the future is by being more mindful in the present. Our failure at being forward-looking may result more from our mindlessness in the present than from any other factor. We operate on automatic pilot, not really noticing what's going on around us, believing that we know everything we need to know, viewing the world through established categories, and operating from a single point of view. Many leaders are not really "present" at all. The body may be in the room, but the mind has been turned off.

To increase our ability to conceive of new and creative solutions to today's problems, we have to stop, look, and listen. We have to *stop doing* for some amount of time each day. We have to remind ourselves that most disruptive electronic devices have an off switch. Turn off the cell phone, the pager, the Instant Messaging, the e-mail, the PDA, and the browser. Stop being in motion.

Then start noticing more of what's going on around you right now. To notice things you have to be present, you have to pay attention, and you have to be curious.

Look around. Most innovation is more a matter of noticing what's going on in the here-and-now than it is of gazing into some crystal ball. The best leaders are and have been those who are the best observers of the human condition. They just pay more attention than everyone else to all that's around them.

Look at the familiar in novel ways. Look for differences and distinctions. Look for patterns. Look at things from multiple perspectives. Look for unmet needs. Listen to the weak signals. Listen to the unheard voices. Listen for things you've never heard before. When we stop, look, and listen we're always amazed at all the possibilities.

Explore Future Possibilities

Even as we stop, look, and listen to messages we're being sent in the present, we also need to raise our heads and gaze out toward the horizon. Being forward-looking is not the same as meeting the deadline for your current project. Whether that project ends three months, one year, five years, or ten years down the road, the leader's job is to think beyond that end date. The leader has to ask, What will we be doing *after* the project is completed? If you're not thinking about what's happening after the completion of your longest-term project, then you're thinking only as long-term as everyone else. In other words, you're redundant! The leader's job is to think about the next project, and the one after that, and the one after that.

And remember. You don't have to do this all by yourself. Just because your constituents expect you to be forward-looking, that doesn't mean you can't ask for help. Our colleague Joel Barker—futurist, author, and filmmaker—uses a historical analogy to provide insight into how leaders can enlist others in their quest to discover what lies ahead. "Before a good wagon master rolled the wagons, he sent out scouts to see what was over the horizon," Joel tells us. "Rapid exploration by scouts provided crucial information that allowed the wagon master to make quicker decisions with higher confidence and move the wagons forward at a faster pace. . . . Twenty-first century leaders need their own scouts. But instead of searching the geography of place, your scouts need to search the geography of time. The most important frontier for you is the next five to 10 years."[1]

Get everyone involved in asking, What's next? Where is this assignment right now taking us *in the future?* And talk out loud about the implications of the things you anticipate. Joel offers this important lesson from his work: "I have found that the most important implications of any change are rarely those that spring immediately from the initiating event, be it an innovation, an emerging trend, the introduction of a competitor's product, a strategic objective. Instead, the most important implications are usually found several orders out from the initiating event. That is, they are the implications of the implications of the implications of the initial event that cascade out in all directions. This is where unintended consequences lurk."

Another crucial question is, What's better? What's better than what you're now doing or anticipate doing in the foreseeable future? The leaders we have talked to share the perspective that helping people find meaning and purpose in their current situations by focusing on making life better in the long run is a key ingredient in getting extraordinary things done.

All enterprises or projects, big or small, begin in the mind's eye; they begin with imagination and with the belief that what's merely an image can one day be made real. To meet our constituents' expectations that we scout the geography of the future, we have no choice as leaders but to take ourselves on journeys in our minds to places we have never been before.

It's imperative that we spend less time on daily operations and more time on future possibilities. This is one of the very few things that makes leadership different from other roles, and it's critical that we make it a priority. It's also where the creation of legacies begins—in the process of deciding how we want the world to be different from what it is today.

CHAPTER 13

It's Not Just the Leader's Vision

At some point during all this talk over the years about the importance of being future-oriented, leaders got the sense that they were the ones who had to be the visionaries. Often with the encouragement of a lot of leadership developers, including us, leaders came to assume that if others expected them to be forward-looking, then they had to go off all alone into the wilderness, climb to the top of some mountain, sit in lotus position, wait for a revelation, and then go out and announce to the world what they foresee. Leaders have assumed that it's their vision that matters, and if it's their vision then *they* have to create it.

Wrong! This is *not* what constituents expect. Yes, leaders are expected to be forward-looking, but they aren't expected to be prescient or clairvoyant. Exemplary leadership is not about uttering divinely inspired revelations. It's not about being a prophet. It's actually much simpler than that.

What people really want to hear is not the leader's vision. They want to hear about *their own* aspirations. They want to hear how their dreams will come true and their hopes will be fulfilled. They want to see themselves in the picture of the future that the leader is painting. The very best leaders understand that their key task is inspiring a *shared* vision, not selling their own idiosyncratic view of the world.

Maybe your constituents don't tell you this quite so directly. Maybe they don't tell you this at all. But we're quite certain that very few adults like to be told in so many words, "Here is where we're going, so get on board with it." No matter how dressed up it is in all kinds of fine and fancy language, most adults don't like being told where to go and what to do. They want to feel part of the process.

Buddy Blanton, a principal program manager at Rockwell Collins Display Systems, learned this lesson firsthand. He got his team together one morning to give him feedback on his leadership approach. He specifically wanted to learn how he could be more effective in creating a shared vision. What they told him helped him understand that it's the process and not just the vision that's critical in getting people all on the same page.

One of the team members that I most respect . . . spoke first. She is very good at telling it like it is, but in a constructive manner. She provided me the following feedback: "You have all of the right skills," she said. "You have global vision and understanding. You are a good, sincere listener. You are optimistic, and you command the respect and trust of your team and your colleagues. You are open and candid, and you are never shy about saying what needs to be said to team members." Then she gave me this advice, "You would benefit by helping us, as a team, to understand how you got to your vision. We want to walk with you while you create the goals and vision so we all get to the end vision together."

Another team member said that sharing this road map would help him to feel more able to take the initiative to resolve issues independently. A couple of other team members stated that this communication would help them to understand the realism of the goals. Other team members said that they would like to be a part of the vision-building process so they could learn how to better build visions for their team.

I looked at the group. It was clear that they were in agreement that they wanted to be a part of the vision sharing and development process. We launched into a discussion on our vision for the program, and each person contributed to the discussion.

Previously, I believed that the team would benefit more by my setting the road map and vision and then just letting them give me feedback when they thought that I was off base—which they have done on numerous occasions. From our discussion, it was clear that the team wants to be included in the process. I asked them if it would be useful if we got together every two weeks to discuss and build our program vision, similar to what we did that day. The feedback was a resounding Yes.

The vast majority of us are just like Buddy's team members. We want to walk *with* our leaders. We want to dream with them. We want to invent with them. We want to be involved in creating our own futures. This doesn't mean you have to do exactly what Buddy did, but it does mean that you have to stop taking the view that vision comes from the top down. You have to stop seeing it as a monologue, and you have to start engaging others in a collective dialogue about the future.

You Have to See What Others See

Take a look at some data for a minute and see what it tells you. On our thirty-item assessment instrument, the Leadership Practices Inventory, six items measure a leader's effectiveness at inspiring a shared vision. Three of the six items are in the bottom four lowest-scoring items, making inspiring a shared vision consistently the leadership practice leaders do least effectively. (The single item at the very bottom of the list is on seeking feedback, something we discussed in Chapter Three of this book.) Here are the three items in question:

- I describe a compelling image of what our future could be like.
- I appeal to others to share an exciting dream of the future.
- I show others how their long-term interests can be realized by enlisting in a common vision.

Examine these three statements for a moment. What do you notice? Do you see that each of these is about how well a leader engages others in the vision? Do you see that these statements are about *us* and not *me, we* and not *I?* The underlying reason for such a poor showing on inspiring a shared vision doesn't seem to be because leaders aren't talking about the future or that they don't have personal convictions about the future. What leaders really struggle with is communicating an image of the future that draws others in—that speaks to what others see and feel.

To be able to describe a compelling image of the future, you have to be able to grasp what *others* want and need. To appeal to others and to show them how their interests will be served, you have to know their hopes, dreams, motives, and interests.

That means you have to know your constituents, and you have to speak to them in language they will find engaging. If you're trying to mobilize people to move in a particular direction, then you've got to talk about the future destination in ways that your audience will find appealing. It's got to be something that they care about as much as you do, or even more.

Getting others excited about future possibilities is not about creating better PowerPoint presentations. It's not about better public speaking skills, although that would help. And it's certainly not about being more charming or charismatic.

It's about intimacy. It's about familiarity. It's about empathy. The kind of communication needed to enlist others in a common vision requires understanding constituents at a much deeper level than we normally find comfortable. It requires understanding others' strongest yearnings and their deepest fears. It requires a profound awareness of their joys and their sorrows. It requires experiencing life as they experience it.

Being able to do this is not magic, nor is it rocket science. It really just calls for listening very, very closely to what other people want.

Now at this point you may be saying to yourself, "All well and good, but what about breakthrough innovations? Aren't leaders supposed to focus on the next new thing? Nobody ever said they wanted an airplane or telephone or personal computer!" True, but people did say they wanted to travel faster to more distant places, connect more easily with their friends and family, and work more productively.

We'd submit that these innovations were not and are not the result of hermits who come up with ideas in isolation. They are, in fact, the result of superb and attentive listening. They are the result of being closely attuned to the environment. They are the result of a greater appreciation of people's aspirations.

And what if people don't know what they need? This is all the more reason to be a stellar listener. Listening is not just about the words. It's also about what is unspoken. It's about reading between the lines. It's about paying attention.

What breakthrough innovators and exemplary leaders understand is that *all* of us want a tomorrow that is better than today. We don't necessarily all want exactly the same thing, but whatever we want, we want it to be an improvement. The critical skill is in discovering just what "new and improved" means to others.

If you're going to stir the souls of your constituents, if you are going to lift them to a higher level of performance, then this is what you need to know: It's not the leader's vision, it's the people's vision that matters most.

CHAPTER 14

Liberate the Leader in Everyone

S ometimes leadership becomes your business unexpectedly, as it did for Mary Beth Phillips, years ago. Her day began like any other, with the family scurrying to get up and about, laundry to do, a walk for the baby, reading to be completed before her afternoon class. Mary Beth left her six-month-old daughter, Elizabeth, at a neighbor's friend's home, to share services of a child-care provider (their own having just moved away), and made her way to graduate school classes. Two hours later, her husband, Bob, was called at work by the nanny, who wondered if the parents ever had a hard time waking the baby up. On intuition, Bob drove to the house to check on Elizabeth and found her in a coma. He immediately drove her to the emergency room at the local hospital, and she was quickly transported to Children's Hospital. Over the next days, weeks, and years they learned that Elizabeth had been shaken so severely that afternoon by her child-care provider that she suffered brain damage and was permanently blinded. Subsequent events revealed aspects of that child-care provider's background that made her quite unsuitable, even dangerous. "Had anyone known, none of us would have left our loved ones in this sick person's hands," Mary Beth explained.

How could this have happened? How could it have been prevented and avoided? What needed to happen so that no other parents, or their children, would experience this nightmare? Mary Beth certainly did not choose this experience, but she took on these questions and led a battle so that parents could have state-conducted criminal and child abuse background checks done on the men and women to whom they were entrusting their loved ones. Mary Beth saw the need and got the State of California to establish TRUSTLINE.

It wasn't easy and it wasn't quick. The journey from Elizabeth's tragedy to the governor's signature, state assembly funding, and implementation by the departments of social services and justice took more than a decade. Mary Beth did it without the benefit of any existing organizational launching pad, formal position, authority, or initial expertise in child welfare. She was driven in her quest, and she eventually involved and mobilized thousands of others along the way. Mary Beth found the leader within her to make certain that no other family would suffer her family's experience.

Even while Mary Beth was leading the TRUST-LINE effort, she wondered how much her reaction to her family nightmare resembled how other parents dealt with, made sense of, and even found some purpose in cruel twists of fate. For her doctoral dissertation, which we served on, she focused on a sample of women, each of whom had, like her, suffered through the sudden and unexpected death or serious injury of her child.

What Mary Beth found was that all these women had become leaders, creating organizations (for example, Vanished Children's Alliance and the Head Trauma Clinic at Children's Hospital in San Diego) and galvanizing people and special interests. Their efforts resulted in new product standards and recalls (new safety requirements for pool covers by the national Consumer Product Safety Commission), social movements (Mothers Against Drunk Driving—MADD), and legislation (California's TRUST-LINE and motorcycle helmet laws).

It seems unlikely that any of these people would have been singled out from the population for their leadership potential. They were mostly young or middle-aged, many were single parents, less than half had graduated from college, many worked at home, and all lacked unique professional credentials or prestigious organizational positions from which to launch their initiatives. They hadn't had any formal (or perhaps even informal) training or special preparation to be leaders. Yet each determined that the situation she experienced would not—must not—happen again for another parent or another child. They got extraordinary things done—and there's no denying the leadership that existed within them—or within each of us.

Like these women, many of the leaders we studied didn't initiate the leadership projects that they wrote and talked about, yet they rose to the occasion. Some got angry and caught fire. Some saw an opportunity where others didn't. Some inherited problems that wouldn't go away and were indeed getting worse. Others accepted an assignment without knowing how dire the situation really was. None of us knows our true strength until challenged to bring it forth. Or as activist and author Rita Mae Brown puts it: "People are like tea bags. You never know how strong they'll be until you put them into hot water."

Leadership Is Learned

Each time we give a speech or conduct a seminar someone invariably asks, "Are leaders born or made?" Our answer, always offered with a smile, is this: "Yes, of course, *all* leaders are born. We've never met a leader who wasn't. So are all accountants, artists, athletes, parents, zoologists, you name it." We're all born. So? It's what you do with what you have before you die that's important. That's the legacy.

It's pure myth that only a lucky few can ever understand the mystery of leadership. Leadership is not a place, and it's not a secret code that can't be deciphered by ordinary people. The truth is that leadership is an observable set of skills and abilities that are useful whether one is in the executive suite or on the front line, on Wall Street or Main Street. And any skill can be strengthened, honed, and enhanced if we have the motivation and desire, practice, and get coaching and feedback.

Of course some people are better at it than others. Again, so what? The more we attribute leadership to a set of innate character traits, the more we abdicate our own responsibility to become the best we can be. The more we wait for genetic scientists to help us select the best and the brightest, the more we avoid personal accountability for the work we must do.

Idan Bar-Sada, engineering vice president at BridgeWave Communications, told us that he had certainly bought into this notion that leadership can't be learned. "I had a few misconceptions about leadership. The main one was that leadership skills, as opposed to management, can't be taught or improved." Then Idan decided to take a leap of faith and get some feedback about how he was doing as a leader. What he learned is instructive to all of us. "I was wrong," he confessed. "With the right knowledge and commitment level, leadership skills can be significantly improved . . . and I'm a case in point!"

It's very curious—and revealing—that no one has ever asked us, "Can *management* be learned? Are *managers* born or made?" Why is it that management is viewed as a set of skills and abilities, while leadership is typically seen as a set of innate personality characteristics? It's simple. People assume management can be learned. Because they do, hundreds of business schools have been established, and each year thousands of management courses are taught. By assuming that people can learn the attitudes, skills, and knowledge associated with good management practices, schools and companies have raised the caliber of managers. They've also contributed to the idea that good management skills are attainable.

In dispelling this myth about leadership being the promise of a select and divine few or that people are hard-wired for leadership you have to set aside the notion that leadership requires a certain personality type. Maryam Mortezazadeh, a manufacturing design engineer at KLA-Tencor, had to do just that. Maryam told us how she once thought leadership meant "charismatic individuals with high energy levels, who like being in the spotlight and can pull many followers behind them—this is just the opposite of what I am." And so Maryam believed she could never be a leader. In fact, a previous manager had told her, when she had expressed some interest in moving into a project management role, that she didn't "possess the gift of leadership because, after all, leaders are born and they are not made."

Through the years Maryam had managed projects with varying levels of difficulty but, she recalls, "I had never thought of myself as a leader, only as a manager." With some coaching she began to see that "leadership is about being able to make a difference." And with this realization, she began to see her own potential. "I too can become a leader, maybe not a charismatic one, but one that can lead others to achieve high outcomes. This realization for me is a major accomplishment." As a result of her new perspective and confidence Maryam has led several professional and personal projects that were stunning successes.

In more than twenty years of research, we've been fortunate to have heard and read the stories of thousands of ordinary people who've led others to get extraordinary things done. Ordinary people whose names are not known and whose stories are not told in the daily news—people like Mary Beth Phillips, Idan Bar-Sada, and Maryam Mortezazadeh—get extraordinary things done on a regular basis. There are millions more. It's not the absence of leadership potential that inhibits the development of more leaders; it's the persistence of the myth that leadership can't be learned. This haunting myth is a far more powerful deterrent to leadership development than is the nature of the person or the basics of the leadership process.

It's our collective task to liberate the leader within ourselves and within every one of us. Rather than view leadership as an innate set of character traits—a self-fulfilling prophecy that dooms society to having only a few good leaders—it's far healthier and more productive to assume that it's possible for everyone to learn to lead. By assuming that leadership is learnable, we can discover how many good leaders there really are. Somewhere, sometime, the leader within each of us will get the call to step forward. By believing in ourselves and by developing our capacity to lead, we'll be prepared when that call comes. And for each time we accept that call, we say yes to one more opportunity to leave a lasting legacy.

CHAPTER 15

Leaders Are Followers, Too!

There's too much focus on the leader leading and not enough on that same leader following.

"A good leader is also a good follower," Susanna Wong, vice president of Sherwood Partners LLC, a business consulting firm in Palo Alto, told us. "This may sound like a paradox," she continued, "but based on my experience I notice that the good leaders are the ones who understand their boundaries and are willing to accept sound advice from their followers." Too many leaders think that they should know it all, be able to do it all, and always be in charge. Susanna reminds us that the best leaders are self-aware enough to realize their limitations and secure enough to know they can let go of control and let others take charge.

It's paradoxical, yes, but the more you demonstrate that you can follow the superior talent of others, the more respect you'll earn. "In my best experiences," Susanna explained, "there wasn't one person dominating the leadership role, regardless of position, but each of us played the leader and the follower at different times. This was a direct result of us recognizing our capabilities." Susanna reminds us that leadership is a dynamic relationship between leaders and followers in which the roles of leader and follower are often exchanged. It's the kind of relationship in which leaders transform followers into leaders.

But if leaders are followers, then what or who exactly is it that they are following? Are they following their direct reports by occasionally giving up their positional power and subordinating themselves to others? Are they following some Big Idea that captivates everyone's imagination? Are they following a set of principles? All of the above? What does it really mean to be a follower?

We Follow a Process and Not a Person

There's precious little discussion of what it really means to be a follower, especially in high-performing organizations. Too often the word *follower* is used pejoratively, implying a possible lack of initiative or drive or ability. It has this connotation of being without a mind of your own. In our own writings we've often been conflicted about using the word *follower,* opting for *constituent* instead because at least it means someone who is an essential participant in something. But what if we let go of this notion that following is something to be disdained, and leadership is all that we should strive to attain? After all, we know that in high-performing teams no one needs to tell anyone else what to do. Everyone understands the vision, the values, what's expected, and how to contribute to making a difference. Everyone's encouraged to do whatever it takes to make things happen. Everyone feels part of the team. Everyone feels authorized and able to take the lead.

The key to high performance is not only good leaders but also good leader*ship.* It's not the person we should be focusing on; it's the process. In the set of skills and abilities, and in the highest-performing organizations, the emphasis is on following the process and not the person. If we were to look at leadership and followership through this lens, here's what we'd be asking people to follow:

- Clear values and beliefs that are consistent with their own.
- A vision of the future that they share.
- Creative ideas that enable the organization to make changes so that the values and vision can be realized.
- Other people whose strengths and talents contribute to the enactment of the values and vision,

and teams whose collective capacity is greater than that of their leaders.

- Their hearts and caring for the people who make it possible to get extraordinary things done.

From this perspective, we are all followers of a way—a way of making a difference in the world. Regardless of our roles in life, we can all exercise leadership when we focus on the principles and practices of leading.

Leaders Follow

Leaders should never get hung up with being "in charge." They should always keep their focus on the destination. They should be asking themselves, Where are we going and how are we planning to get there? Who's the best person at this moment to lead the process of getting us from where we are to where we want to be? Is it me? Or is it another member of our team? Where does the expertise lie? Who's best connected to the sources of information? Who's got the most creative and innovative ideas that'll help us all succeed?

For example, even though Alan Daddow was the person "in charge" at Elders Pastoral in Western Australia, he told us, "I understood that my responsibility was doing whatever I could to maximize the team's effectiveness." Alan realized that success would be achieved if he did what he could do to make everyone else in the organization successful at doing what they needed to accomplish. It was not a matter of what they could do to make him look good.

If leaders kept this in mind then leadership could rotate around the organization. Leaders would be thinking of what's best for the mission, not what's best for themselves. They'd be looking around to find the best fit between people and task. They'd be developing talent so that others could take initiative on their own.

There's another important reason for leaders to follow: no one person can do it alone. The idea of being the leader—the person in charge, the person who's supposed to know everything, the person who's supposed to be able to do anything that's required, the person who's supposed to be better than anyone else, the charismatic bigger-than-life personality, the warrior charging in on a white horse to single-handedly save the day—is daunting. But what happens when we set aside this heroic myth and realize that leaders are not independent of others but, more to the point, dependent upon the energies and efforts of others? Alan Daddow certainly understood this point: "They make me successful. I couldn't accomplish any of this by myself."

You Don't Have to Be the Leader to Lead

Willa McManmon, director of investor relations, Trimble Navigation, had lots of problems with "leaders" early in her career. On the one hand, she thought that being *the* leader was beyond her capabilities. She thought that being the leader meant being perfect, always being right, always knowing what to do, knowing the answers to everyone's questions, and predicting the future with clairvoyance. On the other hand, she thought that being a follower meant that she was simply "the leader's flunky." With experience she came to learn that leading and following were not either-or propositions but related to one another. She told us, "I learned that I am terrific at being 'a leader' when I have the full support and expectations of 'the leader' behind me. I have learned that I can be a follower and a leader in parallel. There is no one more passionate, excited, or committed than I am when I believe in something and someone believes in me. This makes me a terrific leader."

For Willa, as for other leaders, the realization that every one of us is a follower and can also be a leader at the same time is profound. "I believe my strengths lie in this self-awareness," she says, "in my excitement in becoming a better leader and follower, and in my innate sense of determination and fearlessness. The biggest takeaway for me is that I don't have to be perfect to succeed and that I can rely on others to help me, just as they can rely on me to help them. That is a whole new place to start with leading."

Recognizing that leaders follow also means that we don't have to come up with all the good ideas all by ourselves. When we've asked large and small groups "Where do new ideas come from?" there's this moment of awkward silence—as if people think this is some mysterious secret we are about to reveal. And then someone finally shouts, "From our people!" Others chime in: "From our colleagues." "Clients." "Customers." "Suppliers." "Vendors." "Competitors!" In the end, the answer is simply "from all around us." Good process ideas typically come from those doing the work and good product or service ideas come from those using the work. There's really no shortage of ideas, so our task as leaders doesn't require our genius, it requires our listening to and following the ideas of others.

One final thought about appreciating that leaders are followers is the way this perspective contributes to our humility. Unless we truly understand the interdependency between leaders and followers and how leaders themselves need to be followers, then in any quest to leave a legacy we become vulnerable to the sin of hubris. If we come to think of ourselves as "the leader" then we're likely to be blind to what others contribute or deaf to the cries of those around us. We'll come to think of ourselves as better than others—you know, those "little people" around us—and cut ourselves off from their good ideas and their good graces.

Being a follower is good for the soul. It reminds us that we're not alone, that any success we enjoy is dependent upon the success of others, and that we've got to remain open to learning. Humility comes from grasping these fundamental ideas and realizing that our own legacies are built on the legacies of those who have come before us and those who labor alongside us.

PART FOUR

Courage

eaving a legacy is all about making a difference. We can only make a difference when we take stands. Every one of us is capable of taking stands on things that matter. That's what it really means to live a courageous life.

It takes courage to realize your dreams and to give meaning to your values. If you're going to leave a legacy of lasting significance, it'll be the result of acting courageously. You can't plan to be courageous, but you can choose to act that way. Courage is the virtue that makes all other virtues possible.

For most of us, courage is not a matter of grand heroic acts. Personal courage usually means taking the initiative in moments that matter—moments when our core values are challenged. It's doing small things, and those small things can make a huge difference. It's the difference between making a life and just making a living.

Moments of courage are turning points, but we have to be willing to pay a price to earn a return from our lives. Failure is always an option when we want to change the way things are. There is no success without failure, and no learning without mistakes.

Finally, we must realize that leaders never get a money-back guarantee. You can do your best, and it still may simply not be enough. Some forces will always be outside your control. It's also true that every leadership virtue taken to excess can become a vice, and every strength can become a weakness. We have to remain vigilant in reining in our own sense of self-importance, and we must have the humility and grace to admit that we depend on others as much as they depend on us. Each day, nonetheless, brings new opportunities to make a difference in the lives of others, and if we take advantage of these opportunities our legacy will take care of itself.

CHAPTER 16

There's Courage in All of Us

ourage is one of those big, bold words. It has this image of being something way out there on the edges of human experience. It's commonly associated with superhuman feats, life-and-death struggles, and overcoming impossible odds. It has such a mystique about it that many think the concept doesn't apply to them. But when you look beyond the headlines you find out that this account of courage is certainly not the whole story. In fact, it's not even most of the story. It's mostly legend and myth.

Courage, as it turns out, is more common than you might think, is something that everyone has, and it manifests itself daily. It may be precious, but it is not rare. Courage is something within everyone. You may not call on it very often, but it's there when you need it.

Courage Is a State of Mind

One of the first lessons we learned in looking more deeply into courage was that the leadership literature virtually ignores it. For all the talk about how leaders need to be courageous, next to nothing has been written for leaders about what it really means.

That's not to say that no one has ever written or talked about courage. The dialogue on courage is ancient, with most of it among philosophers and historians—and most modern leaders stopped reading philosophy and history after those mandatory classes in school. In this age of quick fixes, if the message can't be reduced to a how-to formula then no one will read the book or attend the lecture.

We also discovered that courage is poorly understood and not what people typically think it is. Courage gives rise to images of daring feats of bravery and nerves of steel, but that's not at all the impression we got in our research or from reading what the philosophers had to say. The ancient Greeks, who did have a lot to say about courage—Socrates and Aristotle, for example—thought of courage as one of four cardinal virtues that were essential for living a good life and for sustaining a civil society. (The others are prudence, temperance, and justice.) Courage, however, sat at the head of the table. It was seen as the grand virtue that made possible all the others.

They spoke of courage as the disposition that gives one the capacity to face danger without being overcome by fear. It's the capacity to persist under highly adverse circumstances. It's not about being fear*less* so much as it is the ability to control fear.

Courage was seen as the mean between the excess of foolhardiness and the deficiency of cowardice. There is such a thing, according to the Greeks—and most of us would agree—as excessive fearlessness. A person who exudes too much confidence in the face of good reason to be fearful is considered rash. These folks are the maniacs among us, and they can be very dangerous. At the same time, fear might be so overwhelming that people run away from what is difficult. These individuals are considered cowards.

The Greeks recognized that people differ. We don't all fear the same things. Therefore, courage is not an absolute. It's relative to the situation and the person. Courage takes form in many different ways. What requires courage from one person might seem easy for another. To the Greeks courage wasn't necessarily about the heroic actions of a warrior in battle. It could also be the determined actions of an ordinary citizen in the pursuit of a better life.

The Greeks also believed that courage wasn't a purely emotional experience—what many call *guts*. Courage, they said, had a rational component. It wasn't just something that you did without thinking. Courage required making a choice in the face of adversity.

The major take-away from our reading of philosophy is that courage is a state of mind. It has to do with how we humans experience certain situations and how we deal with our fears. While there certainly is a physiological component when we encounter adversity, we can make choices about how we handle it. Allowing ourselves to be overwhelmed by fear leaves us with little option but to run. Being too confident that we can handle anything can lead to rashness and foolhardiness. But acknowledging our fears, being appropriately confident that we can handle the situation, and taking initiative despite our fears can be an act of courage.

Everyone Has Moments of Courage

While our reading of philosophy gave us a better sense of the historical meaning, it didn't bring courage alive. So we decided to explore courage by talking to real people about their real experiences. We began asking people to reflect on *moments of courage*—the times in their lives when they believe they demonstrated courage, whatever they understood that word to mean. Those moments of courage could be related to something recent or in the distant past. They could be about something that occurred at work, at school, at home, or in any other setting. The definition and principles emerged from our dialogue.

Many had no problem thinking about a time in their life they had acted with courage, but some struggled with the notion that they had acted courageously. To help these folks get started, we suggested that they begin by completing this sentence: "It took courage for me to—" After completing the sentence several times they settled on something they wanted to talk about. We also told them that their stories didn't require the kinds of heroic acts that make the headlines; we were thinking more about the ordinary, everyday kinds of courage. These personal stories were our entry points into a more intimate understanding of the nature of courage.

So what did we discover? The single most important and striking point was this: *Every single person we interviewed had a story to tell.* Everyone we interviewed could recall an experience that required summoning up courage. Everyone could recall at least one moment in their own lives when they had the mental and moral strength to sustain initiative in a challenging circumstance. Courage is not just for heroes after all.

These conversations also yielded a second critical lesson. The majority of the stories were about everyday encounters with life. They weren't the stereotypical acts of heroism. They weren't monumental life-and-death struggles. The military and paramilitary officers we interviewed didn't tell us about being in the line of fire. The businesspeople we interviewed didn't talk about risking it all on an entrepreneurial venture. The stories were much more mundane—and much more personal. Some were about taking a stand on an important issue. More than one was about speaking in public when stage fright was so bad it made the speaker tremble. Several told us about taking initiative beyond their previous experience levels or comfort zones. A few told us about being lost and finding their way out physically or spiritually. There was a case about outing oneself as a lesbian when working in a conservative financial institution. A few cases were about quitting jobs to go back to school or to make 180-degree career changes. At first our interviewees wondered if their cases really qualified as acts of courage. Yet they found that no other word—*risk-taking,* for example—quite described the quality or character of their experience.

Courage is about making tough choices, but those choices more often than not involve the little things we do. Do I say yes or do I say no? Do I stay or do I leave? Do I speak or do I stay silent? None of these choices on the surface feel particularly frightening, but in the proper context they can be terrifyingly difficult. It's not for anyone to decide whether someone else's act is courageous or not. Ultimately what takes courage and what does not is a very personal decision.

Still, we can make some generalizations. Beneath the veneer of the commonplace were a number of lessons that can teach us all something about what it means to act with courage. Here are some patterns we observed, and although the list may not be complete, it captures most of what we heard. It seems to us that we humans call upon our courage when . . .

- Our lives present some significant challenge, and
- We feel fear when facing this adversity, and
- It requires personal initiative to overcome the fear and the challenge, and
- Something personally meaningful is at stake, and
- We might suffer loss in the process, and
- We have hope, and
- Our life is transformed by the experience.

After telling us their stories people related how their lives were never the same after they had chosen to act. The moment of courage was liberating; it was transformative. Courage was the X Factor in change.

Courage is the virtue that's needed if we're truly going to transform our lives. Courage is the virtue that's needed if we're going to enact anything that is significantly important to us. Courage is the virtue that's needed if we're going to change the status quo.

Leadership is about taking people to places they've never been before, and we can't go to those places without courage. Leadership is *courage in action*. Courage gives us the energy to move forward. Courage gives us the confidence to believe we can make it. Courage gives us the strength to sustain ourselves in the darkest hours. Courage enables us to leave a legacy that declares, "I was here and I made a difference."

CHAPTER 17

You Can't Plan to Be Courageous, But You Can Choose It

People to whom we speak and write always want prescriptions. They want to know how they can apply good ideas to their daily work. Whenever we work with any essential leadership principle, we always try to offer some practical advice. But when it came to advising people on how to become more courageous, we struggled.

In a conversation with author and consultant Peter Block, we asked him for his thoughts on courage. In particular we wanted his opinion on how courage could be made practical for organizations and their leaders. Peter, known for his wisdom, wry wit, and contrarian views, gave us this response: "Courage isn't done for the sake of being practical. It's chosen for its own sake. As soon as you make courage practical, you've stolen its humanity."

Peter's response was a relief. Throughout the entire process of our research on *courage,* we'd had this nagging sense that it didn't lend itself to the usual set of prescriptions and the list of how-to recommendations in management books. Somehow giving in to answering the question about practicality cheapened the value of courage.

But later on in our dialogue, Peter offered this suggestion: "The practical application is to open people up to having the conversation. The action step should be to interview other people about courage in their life. It's an act of love to ask the question, 'In what ways have you been courageous?' because everybody's been courageous in their lives."

That's been our experience. Everyone has a story to tell, and invariably at the end of our conversations people would tell us how *useful* it had been just to talk. Do yourself and others a favor. Open yourself up to the conversation. Take the time to explore the role courage plays in your life. Here are three courage themes you might find useful to explore, because they will enrich your thinking about courage, open up your capacity to act with courage, and possibly provide the spark for leaving your mark.

Conversation 1. Adversities

What in your life or work is causing you great hardship and suffering? What personal or professional issues do you have difficulty discussing with others, and what does this tell you about which situations will require courage from you? When you've dealt with adversity in the past, what did you do that enabled you to get through it successfully?

All acts of courage are associated with adversity and hardship. Severe challenge is always the context surrounding moments of courage. If they were easy, they wouldn't require courage. It may seem obvious that challenge, adversity, difficulty, or danger set the agenda for courage, save for one thing. It's all relative.

Take the case of Beverly Kaye, for instance. Beverly is a highly accomplished businesswoman, author, speaker, and executive educator. One of her moments of courage came early in her life when she was a college dean. She had enrolled as a special postgraduate student at MIT. As Beverly was on her way to the first day of class, she was suddenly overcome with dread. Beverly stuttered very noticeably at times, and she began to imagine that everyone would be asked to make a personal introduction. Then she imagined that when it came her turn she'd stutter over her name, and if she stuttered she was convinced she'd fall apart. So, she turned around in tears and went home.

Fortunately for Beverly, one of her roommates started asking her questions about what would happen if she stuttered. "I kept going through these 'and then whats,'" Beverly told us. "After I ran out of 'and then whats,' I said, 'Well, I'll somehow get out my name, say who I am, and what I do, and then eventually it will be the next person's turn.' And with that statement, 'and then it will be the next person's turn,' I realized I wouldn't roll over dead, people wouldn't shun me, and they wouldn't throw me out. It would be someone else's turn, and I would just have to get through that rough spot. . . . with the knowledge that I could stutter, it would be over eventually, and then people would come to know me and love me. You know, it gave me the courage to keep going."

For most of us saying our name and talking about ourselves in class is a piece of cake, but then most of us never have to suffer the trauma of stuttering badly in public. Beverly did. For her, it was an excruciating challenge to stand in front of her peers and say her name.

Moments of courage are moments of truth. They are those critical incidents in our lives when we come face-to-face with who we are and what we are made of. They are self-revealing moments, or as one executive said to us: "Adversity introduces you to yourself." By honestly opening up about our adversities, we are getting to know ourselves.

Conversation 2. Fears

What are you most afraid of? What terrifies you? Why are you afraid, terrified, apprehensive, or distressed?

Media portrayals of courage make it seem as if being fear*less* and being courageous are synonyms. We may even get the sense that if we're afraid, then we can't possibly have courage. But nothing could be further from the truth. Fear and courage go hand in hand.

Consultant and author John Izzo expresses it this way: "Part of courage is to face whatever are the inner blocks or demons or barriers that keep you from becoming the fullest person you can be in the world. A lot of courage is really facing yourself." In relating one of his moments of courage, John said, "I knew I had to confront that fear of the unknown, of truly of being on my own, of just going to a place where I knew no one, where I had no idea really what I was getting into. . . . In a way, I broke the bonds of almost all of my fears by confronting that one fear, which was of taking a risk of the unknown, of not playing it safe."

Moments of courage can be unpleasant. We may even anticipate great danger and harm. The anxieties are unique to the person and the situation, which is why no two cases of courage are ever exactly the same. Yet there is the common thread of confronting one personal demon or another.

There is no such thing as acting courageously and feeling no fear or sense of potential loss. Fear is what makes the conversation real. As Peter Block put it to us, "When you feel fear it's the moment you're most alive. It's a sign of life." The courage point is where fear meets danger. It's that intersection that we need to explore. We have to move toward it. We have to embrace it. Despite the fear and in spite of the darkness, we have to act.

Conversation 3. Suffering

When you think about the adversities that you face, what's at stake? How ready are you to face your fears? How ready are you to suffer for your cause?

In each of the cases we gathered on moments of courage, something significant was at stake. There was the potential for loss—of careers, jobs, money, friends, or face. When you step into the zone of courage you're exposed. You're hanging out there. You're not playing it safe. The consequences can be severe, or at least they feel that way at the time.

Jim "Gus" Gustafson, a leadership researcher and wireless company executive, realized that in order to pursue his dream, he needed to quit his job. He couldn't do it justice unless he gave 100 percent of the same kind of passion and energy that he was putting into his work.

"I'd been employed since I was tall enough to push a lawnmower," he said, "and the concept of walking away from a perfectly good job was frightening. I had two little kids at home and a wife that was a stay-at-home mom. To go from a really nice comfortable income to zero income and no health insurance and everything that goes along with that was absolutely terrifying to me. And yet, it was just something I knew in my heart and in my gut I needed to go do, or it would never get done."

If there's one thing that seems to stop us from acting courageously, it's our unwillingness to suffer. We're not always ready, but nonetheless courage doesn't occur without some degree of suffering and loss. Sometimes it's temporary and will pass, but other times it may persist for years. Before we can act with great courage we have to be mentally, emotionally, and physically prepared to make sacrifices.

You can't plan to be courageous. No one told us that on a particular moment, on a particular day they intended to be courageous. But you can choose it. Engaging in conversations about your own and others' life struggles is one crucial way to begin preparing for that choice.

CHAPTER 18

It Takes Courage to Make a Life

The Reverend Peter J. Gomes writes, "We would like to make a life and not just a living, which—as we all know from our own experience and that of others—takes courage."[1] We may be able to make a living—and a very secure and comfortable one at that—without exercising courage. Yet most of us want more from life than security and comfort. We also want a life full of meaning and significance. We want a life that matters, a life that makes some kind of difference to our family and friends, and even possibly to our organizations, our communities, and our world. It takes courage to make that kind of life. It takes courage to make a lasting difference.

Rosa Parks, receiving a gesture normally reserved for titans of government, lay in state in the rotunda of the U.S. Capitol building before her funeral. More than fifty years ago she quietly showed us just how courage can make a life and in the process set in motion a series of events that changed the course of history. Looking back and reflecting on her actions teaches us three very important lessons about courage, leadership, and living a life that leaves a legacy.

Lesson One: Little Acts Can Have Huge Impact

On the first day of December 1955 the bus driver of the Cleveland Avenue bus in Montgomery, Alabama, demanded that black riders move from their seats in the racially neutral middle section of the bus to make way for white passengers. Rosa Parks, one of those black riders, remained seated. When he asked her directly if she was going to stand up, she said, "No, I am not." When he told her that if she didn't move he'd have her arrested, she said, "Go ahead."[2]

Rosa Parks's actions weren't strategic or grand. They weren't self-promotional or manipulative. They weren't complex or superhuman. They were simple and mundane. In the context of the times, Rosa Parks's actions and the ensuing courtroom proceedings certainly had all the elements of high drama. It was an extremely tense and potentially explosive situation. But when you closely examine Rosa Parks's actual behaviors—not moving, saying no, willingly getting arrested—they're actions that each and every one of us has the personal resources to take. They don't require big budgets, off-site strategic retreats, endless planning sessions, or huge armies. They require only a personal decision and the will to stick with it. It's stunning to realize how small things can have such large impact.

Just look at the impact of the little things she did. When she said no and refused to move, she gave momentum to a movement. Her gesture of defiance precipitated a yearlong protest and boycott, helped to elevate the young Martin Luther King Jr. to prominence, and infused new energy into the civil rights movement. Her actions mobilized people suddenly and quickly into a whole new level of activity.

Lesson Two: One Person Can Make a Difference

By her refusal to move from her seat, Rosa Parks demonstrated the power of one person. She showed us all that it's possible for one human being to make a difference. She showed us that each of us matters in this life on this earth.

Rosa Parks was not a powerful or important civil rights leader. She was not a visible activist. She was a seamstress on her way home from work. She was a wife, member of her church congregation, good neighbor, and a volunteer in the army of black citizens doing their part.

Rosa Parks is a stirring example of how we all have the potential to change the world—or at least a little piece of it. She exemplifies exactly what we mean when we say that leadership is everyone's business.

Lesson Three: Courageous Acts Flow from Beliefs

Courageous acts flow from a commitment to deeply held beliefs—you just can't separate the two. "I didn't get on the bus that day to get arrested. I got on the bus to go home," she writes in her autobiography, *Quiet Strength*. "It's funny to me how people came to believe that the reason that I did not move from my seat was that my feet were tired. My feet were not tired, but *I* was tired of unfair treatment."[3]

Rosa Parks's refusal to move was an act of courage that emerged from within. "There had to be a stopping place," she said, "and this seemed to have been the place for me to stop being pushed around and to find out what human rights I had, if any."[4] Rosa Parks was committed to deeply rooted beliefs, to a set of guiding principles that were not only dear to her but also at the very core of a nation. She decided that day in December to test the truth of those fundamental ideals.

Rosa Parks Moments

We've come to refer to this type of action—small but with high impact, requiring personal initiative, and decisively rooted in values—as a Rosa Parks Moment, or RPM. Just like that other use of the RPM acronym—Revolutions Per Minute—Rosa Parks Moments are about movement, about turning something around. It seems a fitting reference since Rosa Parks's simple act of standing . . . excuse us, sitting . . . on principle was one of the forces that started things spinning faster during the civil rights movement.

But I'm not Rosa Parks, you say. Well, get this. Rosa Parks wasn't the Rosa Parks we celebrate today until *after* she did what she did. Before that she was a seamstress and a citizen. Before that she was just like the rest of us. Not famous and not wealthy and not a hero. It was her courageous actions that made the difference. She could have moved, but she didn't. She could have stayed silent, but she didn't.

This is a powerful lesson we all need to heed. It's the Rosa Parkses of the world that truly make the difference, and we are all Rosa Parks. We all have the capacity to create Rosa Parks Moments. A Rosa Parks Moment is generated when you apply initiative (I) to a core value's challenge (CVC). If it were a formula, it'd look something like this: $I \times CVC = RPM$.

When someone or something challenges one of your deeply held beliefs and you grab hold of that opportunity right then and there to confront it, you have a Rosa Parks Moment. The value doesn't have to be something as monumental as freedom and justice, but it does have to be something that is extraordinarily important to you. It has to be a time when you say to yourself, "Enough is enough. I'm not going to take it anymore." And you have to be resolute about it. No fence sitting. No hemming and hawing. No equivocating. This is the moment; this is the time when you *have to* act. When that young man in Tiananmen Square stood alone in front of the government's tank, he was exercising a Rosa Parks Moment.

Rosa Parks Moments are turning points in our lives. They may even become turning points in other people's lives. The greater the number of people who resolutely seize that moment when core values are challenged, the greater the likelihood that individual lives will be improved and organizations and communities will be renewed. You never really know what might become a legacy.

Significant and lasting change depends on Rosa Parks Moments. Significant and lasting change depends on individuals' taking initiative to confront challenges to core values. Significant and lasting change depends on you.

So we all have to ask ourselves, When was my last RPM? When was the last time I fought for a value that I cherished? When was the last time I was resolute in the face of stern resistance? And we also have to ask ourselves, am I ready for my next RPM? We never really know when we'll be asked to abandon a value we hold dear, but we have to be prepared for when it might happen.

The challenges that confront us in these troubled times aren't going to evaporate like fog on a summer morning. They require a lot more of us if we're to overcome them. They demand that we make tough choices. They demand that we make sure we're clear about what we value and believe in. They demand that we take personal initiative when those values are challenged. They demand that we focus on the little things we do each day to be true to ourselves. They demand resilience and determination.

Rosa Parks showed us that each and every one of us matters. She showed us that even the very simplest of actions could ripple through society, creating waves of change. She showed us how courage can make a life. She showed us how we each can leave a lasting legacy.

CHAPTER 19

The Courage to Be Human

Leadership is a humbling experience. Whenever anyone asks us about our own leadership practices, we're quick to admit that leadership is hard work, and that it's a lot easier to write about leadership than it is to do it. A review of our own published lists of things that people need to do to be better leaders often feels like a long and discouraging reminder of personal shortcomings.

Anyone who's ever been in a leadership role quickly learns that you're squeezed between others' lofty expectations and your own personal limitations. You realize that while others want you to be of impeccable character, you're not always without fault. You learn that you can't see around every corner, and even if you know your way forward everyone may not end up at the same destination, let alone be on time. You discover that despite your best efforts to introduce brilliant innovations, most of them don't succeed. You find that you sometimes get angry and short, and that you don't always listen carefully to what others have to say. You're reminded that you don't always treat everyone with dignity and respect. You recognize that others deserve more credit than they get, and that you've failed to say thank you. You know that sometimes you get, and accept, more credit than you deserve.

In other words, you realize that you're human.

The words *human* and *humble* share a common origin. They both come from the Latin *humus*, meaning earth. To be human and humble is to be down-to-earth, both feet planted firmly on the ground. Interesting, isn't it, how as people climb the ranks in organizations they also climb to a higher floor in the building, getting farther and farther away from the ground? It gets harder and harder to remain humble the higher up you go.

The Courage to Be Humble

The courage to be human is the courage to be humble. It takes a lot of courage to admit that you aren't always right, that you can't always anticipate every possibility, that you can't envision every future, that you can't solve every problem, that you can't control every variable, that you aren't always congenial, that you make mistakes, and that you are, well, human. It takes courage to admit all these things to others, but it may take even more courage to admit them to yourself. If you can find the humility to do that, however, you invite others into a courageous conversation. When you let down your guard and open yourself up to others, you invite them to join you in the creation of something that you alone could not create. When you become more modest and unpretentious, others have the chance themselves to become visible and noticed.

Film director Sidney Lumet, whose legacy includes such cinematic greats as *12 Angry Men* and *Network,* understands that even when we are, supposedly, in charge, we are still beholden to many factors outside our domain. It's a humbling experience, but also one that can bring great joy to the endeavor. In talking about his role as a director, he says:[1]

> But how much in charge am I? *Is the movie un Film de Sidney Lumet?* I'm dependent on weather, budget, what the leading lady had for breakfast, who the leading man is in love with. I'm dependent on the talents and idiosyncrasies, the moods and egos, the politics and personalities, of more than a hundred different people. And that's just in making the movie. At this point I won't even discuss the studios, financing, distribution, marketing, and so on.
>
> So, how independent am I? Like all bosses—and on the set, I'm the boss—I'm the boss only up to a point.

And to me that's what's so exciting. I'm in charge of a community that I need desperately and that needs me just as badly. That's where the joy lies, in the shared experience. Anyone in the community can help me or hurt me.

That was just in making the movie, and didn't include all the other aspects of the business. Leadership in all settings is just like that. You will never, ever find, in historic or present times, even one example of a leader who controlled every aspect of the environment. And you'll never find an example of a leader who enlisted 100 percent of the constituents in even the most compelling of future possibilities. Not only is this realistic, it's fortunate. We should all be grateful for the forces we can't control and the voices we can't enlist. We need the cynics, skeptics, and alternative voices to keep our freedom. We need the challenges, surprises, and adversities to strengthen our courage and unleash our resolve.

Modesty may not seem like an important leadership virtue these days, but failure to keep your feet planted firmly on the ground invariably leads to the greatest leadership sin of all—hubris. Excessive pride has gotten more than a fair share of leaders and companies in a heap of trouble. It's gotten so bad in corporate America that a number of people are embarrassed to admit to being a corporate executive. We asked a group of youngsters the other day if they knew the names of companies and their list included Enron, WorldCom, Tyco, and Calpine. Clearly these firms are not being remembered for their greatness, but for their leaders' excesses. In a 2005 Gallup Poll only 16 percent of the public rated business executives as very high on honesty and ethics. Compare that with 82 percent for nurses and 7 percent for telemarketers.[2]

Our friend and colleague Kirk Hanson, university professor and executive director of the Markkula Center for Applied Ethics at Santa Clara University, asserts that the Achilles' heel of leaders can be found when they

- Believe they know it all.
- Believe they are in charge.
- Believe the rules don't apply to them.
- Believe they will never fail.
- Believe they did it all by themselves.
- Believe they are better than the "little people."
- Believe they *are* the organization.
- Believe they can focus everything on the job.

We have to recognize that however smart we are we're not smarter than everyone else combined. We have to appreciate that not only do the same rules apply to us, perhaps they apply even more because our behavior is seen as setting the standard for others. We have to be vigilant in noticing our mistakes and admitting them before they're printed in the press. We can't lose sight of the fact that no matter how important our own contributions are, we couldn't have gotten anywhere without the help and hard work of lots of other people.

We have to remember our roots—that we didn't start out at the top of the pyramid or in the front of the line, and that often we're afraid, intimidated, uncertain, tentative, and even anxious. We have to have enough sense of self to not get lost in our jobs and to not let work become 24/7 (no matter how much technology may enable that to happen).

The Need for More Grace in the Workplace

The people we work with and count on are also human, and despite their best intentions they don't always do what they say they will do. We need to give them the same opportunities we afford ourselves to try and fail and try again. We need to give them the chance to be the best they can be, even to be better than they thought they could be. We need to support them in their growth and help them to recognize that the journey is not about perfection but about becoming fully human.

In the Academy Award–winning film *As Good as It Gets* (1997), featuring Helen Hunt and Jack Nicholson, a single mother and waitress forms an unlikely relationship with an obsessive-compulsive, misanthropic author. In one unforgettable scene, nearly halfway through the film, they are sitting together in a restaurant and Carol (played by Hunt) pleads with Melvin (played by Nicholson) to "say something nice." Melvin responds with a completely unexpected comment. "You make me want to be a better man." Carol is blown away and clearly touched by Melvin's graciousness. She says, "That's maybe the best compliment of my life."

Isn't that what it's really all about? Melvin *was* paying Carol a great compliment, and he was also speaking the truth about how we are all affected by a person who is truly gracious. Isn't that what the truly great leaders do? Don't they touch us this way, making us say to ourselves: "I want to be in this relationship with you because being in this relationship brings out the best in me and makes me want to be and do all that I am capable of. You see greatness in me that I don't even realize. And you care for me even when I am not at my best." Isn't that also what love is all about?

What if grace had been more present in those organizations that are now so infamous for their hubris and greed? What if they had lived by the philosophy that leaders are here to make people want to be better people and not just want to make more money? What if all leaders started each day asking themselves, "In every interaction today, considering all the people I interact with, what one thing can I do to make them better?"

We could all use a bit more grace in the world these days. We could use more good will, more charm, more elegance, and more thanksgiving. We could also use more forgiveness—starting with forgiving ourselves for our own limitations and shortcomings. But let's not stop there. We have to extend that same compassion to others. Leaders aren't saints. They're human beings, full of the same flaws and failings as the rest of us. This is not a recommendation to coddle the corporate criminals, only a suggestion that, in the course of living our lives as courageously as we can, we will all fail, and sometimes we'll fail miserably. Forgiveness can lighten that heavy burden just a little bit.

Humility and grace make up the antidote to the poison of excessive pride and the rapacious harm that it does to our lives. It would serve us all well to keep a dose of it handy as we deal with the complex challenges and lurking temptations of our modern organizations.

Let's all have the humility to remember where we started and the humanity to offer others the same opportunities. When the time comes for them to speak of your legacy, is there anything better to be remembered for than "You made me want to be a better person"?

CHAPTER 20

Failure Is Always an Option

In our work we talk about how leaders, to create a climate that fosters innovation, should not punish failure and mistakes when people are trying something new and different. Instead, when things do not go as expected, they should always ask, What can we learn?

In one recent group discussion a participant challenged this perspective: "Well then, what do you think about the statement you hear from some executives that 'failure is not an option'?" We could all picture some macho drill sergeant yelling this out to a bunch of new recruits or some self-assured executive bellowing loudly to a new product team.

Our reply was pretty abrupt and quick. "'Failure is not an option,'" we said, "is one of the dumbest clichés ever uttered. It ranks right up there with 'get it right the first time,' another well-intended management nostrum that just encourages people to play it safe."

Telling people that failure is not an option is just plain nonsense. Failure is always an option. In real life, when we're trying to do something we've never done before, we virtually never get it right the first time. And if we do, it's sheer luck. In real life, we make lots of mistakes when doing something new and different. In real life, failure is always an option.

We'd go even further. If you're not *willing* to fail at what you do, you'll *never* become great and you'll never innovate. The actor Jeff Daniels makes just this point when talking about accepting the role of novelist Bernard Berkman in the 2005 film *The Squid and the Whale*. "I took the role," he says, "because I didn't know how to do it. It was new, it was unpredictable, and there was a chance to fail."[1]

But don't listen to us or to an actor about greatness, listen instead to basketball legend Michael Jordan. One of the best ever to play the game, Jordan once observed, "I've missed more than nine thousand shots in my career. I've lost three hundred games. Twenty-six times I've been trusted to take the winning shot and missed. I've failed over and over again in my life. And that is why I succeed."[2]

Listen also to James E. West, research professor at Johns Hopkins University, who has secured fifty domestic and more than two hundred foreign patents. "I think I've had more failures than successes, but I don't see the failures as mistakes because I always learned something from those experiences. I see them as having not achieved the initial goal, nothing more than that."[3]

Professionals Believe in Possibilities

It's really all about your point of view. Imagine that you play professional baseball. You know the statistics of the game. The very best hitters each season will have a batting average of a little bit better than .300. For every ten times they get up to bat, they get about three hits. So if you were a pro baseball player getting ready to take your turn at the plate, what would you be thinking? "Well, let's see," you could say to yourself. "Being the professional that I am, I know that the most likely thing that's going to happen to me is that I won't get a hit. I'm going to be out." Given this attitude—a very realistic one given the nature of the game—you could then resign yourself to the outcome and say, "Why, then, should I even bother stepping up to the plate? Or if I do, why should I pay much attention or swing very hard?" We all know that's not what you're going to do. You're going to do your best to get a hit.

The real reality is that despite the probabilities, professionals believe in the possibilities. They get up to bat every single time believing that they will get a hit. They focus, unshoulder the bat, and swing. And you know what? Sometimes they succeed.

It's the same for leaders. The statistics tell us that most innovations fail the first few times. But does the failure rate stop exemplary leaders from innovating? No. Why? Because there's always a 100 percent *possibility* of success. It's not about failing or succeeding. It's about doing. The more attempts, the more chances to get a hit.

What's truly paralyzing about the notion that failure is not an option is that it increases the pressure to avoid experimentation and never do anything risky. The fears and anxieties that are produced by this perspective are magnitudes greater than those experienced when the attitude is that the only way to succeed is to try. Unless we're willing to try something that we have never tried before, progress simply won't happen. We will not move forward, either as organizations or as individuals. We'll be stuck in one place, going through the motions, locked into an activity trap that associates keeping busy with making progress.

A Learning Curve Is Not a Straight Line

Here's another way to think about it. Let's say you're doing something right now that you know how to do.

Then someone comes along and suggests that there's a better way. Your initial reaction might be "Well that's fine but the way I'm now doing it works well enough, and I'm comfortable doing it this way." But that's not how progress or learning happens. We only learn and move forward when we experiment and experience doing differently what we already know how to do well.

It's called a learning curve. A learning curve is not a straight line. It always goes down before it goes up— and should it ever go up first then you're only measuring something you already knew how to do but weren't doing!

Better yet, consider the case when you can say to yourself, "I don't know how to do this, and I would like to be able to." There's no other choice in this instance but to learn. Telling yourself to get it right the first time is a ridiculous standard to set, because you won't. The real issue is how *fast* can you learn? How quickly can you learn from your mistakes and your failures before you get it right? Picture that learning curve in your head, and you'll know why most innovations are failures in the middle. Perseverance is the hallmark of innovators— and leaders.

The truth is that failures and disappointments are inevitable. It is how you handle them that will ultimately determine your effectiveness and success. You have to be honest with yourself and with others. You have to own up to your mistakes and reflect on your experiences so that you gain the learning necessary to be better the next time around. Resilience is critical to leadership and learning.

There's an additional payoff. You gain credibility when you admit you make mistakes and aren't perfect. It may sound counterintuitive, but that's precisely what Hasan Ertas, a senior design engineer at Stryker Endoscopy, explained to us: "I realized that whether I admit that I made a mistake or not, other people find out about it and they know. So, I decided, why don't I save them the time and trouble and save dignity for myself and admit my mistakes up front." The result for Hasan was unexpected: "Interestingly, when this happens people will back you up and support you even beyond necessary."

Hasan also related another equally important lesson he learned. "I feel that if you can accept your own mistakes then you are more likely to understand and accept others' mistakes as well. And this makes other people feel more secure and trusting around you. They will work very hard for you without fearing mistakes because they know that you have done the same thing and it's okay to make mistakes as long as you work genuinely hard to correct and learn from them."

Life is our laboratory, and we ought to use it to conduct as many experiments as possible. Try, fail, learn. Try, fail, learn. Try, fail, learn. That should be the leader's mantra. Charles Kettering, the founder of Delco and holder of more than 140 patents, used to say, "It doesn't matter if you try and try and try again, and fail. It does matter if you try and fail, and fail to try again." We should all heed his advice. History will not judge us harshly for our failures if we learn from them, but it will be unkind to us if we fail to try, and if we fail to learn. It seems to us that those who have left the most lasting legacies are those who have failed but then tried again, for it's that final try that makes all the difference.

CHAPTER 21

No Money-Back Guarantee

News Flash: You can do all this leadership stuff perfectly and still get fired!

Take the case of a friend of ours, a former senior vice president of marketing for a large packaged goods company. Several years ago he faced a critical leadership challenge. New technology made it possible to introduce a substitute for his company's product. Major customers were shifting to the substitute. His market studies clearly indicated that the future of the industry lay in the new product. He was convinced that his company had to revise its long-range plans and develop its own entry into the market or suffer disastrous consequences.

He took his studies to the board and urged development of a market entry. The board did not share his point of view. It authorized its own independent investigations by two prestigious management consulting firms to determine market trends and technical feasibility of producing the product. To the board's surprise, the consulting reports supported the senior vice president's sense of the market. Still unconvinced but now a bit worried, the board asked two law firms to determine whether entry into the new market would pose any antitrust issues. Both sets of lawyers agreed there would be no problem.

Despite the overwhelming evidence that the senior vice president's strategic vision was clear and attainable, the board sought the opinion of yet a third law firm. This one gave the board the answer it had apparently been looking for all along. The company abandoned the pursuit of the new product. The senior vice president, however, could not in good conscience go along with the decision—to him it was a matter of integrity. He felt so strongly about his vision for the industry that he continued to pursue it. Despite an untarnished reputation and a superb track record, he could not persuade his management to undertake a new strategic direction, and they fired him.

We know this senior vice president very well. He excels as a leader. He's someone we've held up as a role model for others to follow. Even so, he got fired. That's the messy reality of leadership. Sometimes, despite our very best efforts and our very best intentions, we don't succeed.

Perhaps we should have told you this sooner, but it's our guess that you knew it already. You knew it from your personal experience, or you knew it from the experience of those close to you. You knew it because no one can ever be *that* good.

There are no get-rich-quick, instant weight-loss programs for leaders. There's absolutely no way that any expert can claim that you can be successful all the time with all the people. And if any gurus ever stand in front of you and assert—or if any authors, including us, ever write—that they have *the* three-, five-, seven-, or nine-factor theory that's 100 percent guaranteed to get you certain results and rewards or-your-money-back, then grab onto your wallet and run away as fast as you can. You're about to be sold a bill of goods. None of us will ever get everything right. And even if we were so lucky, the project could still fail, people could still get laid off, and we could still get fired.

Strengths Can Become Weaknesses

There's something else we should confess. Any leadership practice *can* become destructive. Virtues can become vices. Strengths can become weaknesses.

We know, for example, that finding your voice and setting an example are essential to credibility and accomplishment. But an obsession with being seen as a role model can lead to being too focused on your own values and your way of doing things. It can cause you to discount others' views and be closed to feedback. It can push you into isolation for fear of losing privacy or being "found out"; it can also cause you to be more concerned with style than substance. Shared values can also become straitjackets, consensus on norms can become groupthink, and communities can become cults that limit free choice.

We know that being forward-looking and communicating a clear and common vision of the future are what set leaders apart from others. Yet a singular focus on one vision of the future can blind a leader to other possibilities as well as to the realities of the present. It can cause you to miss the exciting possibilities that are just out of your sight or make you hang on just a little too long to an old, tired, out-of-date technology. Exploiting your powers of inspiration can cause others to surrender their will. Your own energy, enthusiasm, and charm may be so magnetic that others don't think for themselves. Being overly upbeat can blind you to the hard realities that we all face.

We realize that challenging the process is essential to promoting innovation and progressive change. Seizing the initiative and taking risks are necessary for learning and continuous improvement. But taken to extremes, they create needless turmoil, confusion, and paranoia. Routines are important, and if people rarely get the opportunity to gain confidence and competence through repetition they'll lose their motivation to try new things. Change for change's sake can be just as demoralizing as complacency.

We understand that collaboration and teamwork are essential to getting extraordinary things done in today's world. Innovation depends on high degrees of trust. And people must be given the power to be in control of their own lives if they are to accomplish great things. But an overreliance on collaboration and trust may reflect an avoidance of critical decisions or cause errors in judgment. Too much polling and too much listening can turn into indecisiveness and inconsistency; it can become just crowd-pleasing and not leading. It may be a way of *not* taking charge when the situation requires it. Delegating power and responsibility can become a way of dumping too much on others when they're not fully prepared to handle it.

We know that people perform at higher levels when they're appreciated and encouraged. Personal recognition and group celebration create the spirit and momentum that can carry a group forward even during the toughest of challenges. At the same time constantly worrying about who should be recognized and when to celebrate can turn leaders into gregarious minstrels. We can lose sight of the mission because we're having so much fun. We can become so consumed by all the perks and pleasures that we forget the purpose of it all.

So What Should We Do?

At this point you may be asking, "If there's no way we can get it perfect, and if we do happen to excel at it we can overdo it, what should I do?" If perfection is not the leadership ideal, what is?

The answer is *being more of who we are*. Our colleague David Whyte—author and poet—once said, "The great question of leadership, about taking real steps on the pilgrim's path, is the great question of any individual life: how to make everything more personal."[1] We each have certain gifts to offer, certain talents to share, certain contributions to make. Taking the lead gives us a chance to make those public. It gives us a chance to define ourselves and in the process offer our best selves to others. It gives us a chance to shape our own life and also to share in the shaping of others. It gives us a chance to assert a point of view and see if others share similar dreams and aspirations. It gives us the chance to present something that's important to us, and by doing so add value to the lives of others. It gives us the chance to make a difference.

Our challenge is to stay focused on the difference we want to make, why we think it's essential to be moving in that direction, and on the people who will come after us to inherit what we leave. If we stay focused on the difference and the people, the legacy will take care of itself.

Afterword

The Legacy You Leave Is the Life You Lead

We were humbled when Sergey Nikiforov, a Russian immigrant to the United States who is co-founder and vice president of product development at Stack3, Inc., wrote this note to us:

> Where do I start becoming a better leader? This question has been nagging me for some time. Naively I assumed that to become a better leader meant to perform formidable tasks: moving mountains, saving lives, changing the world for the better. As you have pointed out these noble, grandiose tasks are often insurmountable for a single person.
>
> Then it occurred to me—I was thinking selfishly. What I envisioned was instant gratification, recognition for my skills and talent. Although the issues at work matched well with your book's materials, the

way I dealt with them was far from ideal. In most cases, I used wrong tools and methods.

I found that every day I had an opportunity to make a small difference. I could have coached someone better, I could have listened better, I could have been more positive toward people, I could have said "thank you" more often, I could have . . . the list just went on. At first, I was a bit overwhelmed with the discovery of how many opportunities I had in a single day to act as a better leader. But as I have gotten to put these ideas into practice I have been pleasantly surprised by how much improvement I have been able to make by being more conscientious and intentional about acting as a leader.

Sergey has nailed it. Each day provides countless chances to make a difference. The chance might come in a private conversation with a direct report or in a meeting with colleagues. It might come over the family dinner table. It might come when you're speaking at a conference on the future of your business, or it might come when you're listening to a friend talk about a current conflict with a peer. There are many moments each day when you can choose to lead and many moments each day when you can choose to make a difference. Each of these moments serves up the prospect of contributing to a lasting legacy.

When we choose to lead every day, we choose to serve. Leading is not about what we gain from others but about what others gain from us. This means we have to be prepared to sacrifice, to teach, to learn, to remain open to honest feedback, and to never, ever assume that the leader can do it alone.

When we choose to lead every day, we reenlist in a very special relationship with others. We enlist a relationship that's uniquely personal. Contrary to what you may have been told before, leaders *should* want to be liked. People just won't do their best for leaders with whom they don't feel a caring connection. But leaders don't want a climate where everyone always sees eye to eye. Constructive conflict is essential to creativity and innovation. Yet all human relationships are based on trust, and a lack of cohesiveness makes relationships vulnerable. We can never take trust for granted. We have to earn it, build it, and sustain it every day. Where there's a climate of trust, there's also a climate in which leaders can let go of control and grant everyone ownership of their own actions.

When we choose to lead every day, we choose aspirations of long-term significance over short-term measures of success. While looking forward may be the quality that differentiates leaders from other credible people, the future does not belong to leaders alone. Leaders are its custodians; their constituents are its occupants. The occupants have to have a role in shaping where they will live. That means that leaders have to turn their followers into leaders, and leaders also have to be willing to become followers themselves.

All this takes great courage. It takes courage to lead. It takes courage to make a life. Courage, like leadership, is a choice. We may not know when we'll be called upon to be courageous, and we may not know when we'll be called upon to lead. But, when the moment comes when we must choose, we should take heart that there's courage in everyone. We will not always succeed—there are no guarantees in leadership or life—but the courage to be human will keep us humble and keep us strong.

As our colleague John Maxwell, himself the author of numerous books on leadership, told us, "It's been said that there are two kinds of people in life: those who make things happen and those who wonder what happened. Leaders have the ability to make things happen. People who don't know how to make things happen for themselves won't know how to make things happen for others." He went on to tell us, "What you do with the future means the difference between leaving a track record and leaving a legacy."

Legacies aren't the result of wishful thinking. They're the result of determined doing. The legacy you leave is the life you lead. We lead our lives daily. We leave our legacy daily. The people you see, the decisions you make, the actions you take—they are what tell your story. It's the sum of everything you do that matters, not one large bequest at the end of your tenure. Despite all our talk about leaders' needing to be concerned about the future, the most important leadership actions are the ones you take today.

You just never know whose life you might touch. You just never know what change you might initiate and what impact you might have. You just never know when that critical moment might come. What you do know is that you can make a difference. You can leave this world better than you found it.

Notes

CHAPTER 1

1. John W. Gardner, *On Leadership* (New York: Free Press, 1990), pp. 28–29.
2. Robert Greenleaf, *Servant Leadership: A Journey into the Nature of Legitimate Power and Greatness* (New York: Paulist Press, 1977), p. 7.

CHAPTER 2

1. Peter F. Drucker, "My Mentors' Leadership Lessons," in *Leader to Leader: Enduring Insights on Leadership from the Drucker Foundation's Award-Winning Journal,* edited by Frances Hesselbein and Paul M. Cohen (San Francisco: Jossey-Bass, 1999), p. 4.

CHAPTER 3

1. Ralph Keyes, *The Courage to Write: How Writers Transcend Fear* (New York: Henry Holt, 1995), p. 37.

2. Dan Mulhern, "Do You Really Know What They Think?" In "Reading for Leading: A Weekly Stimulant for Those Who Lead," December 12, 2005. Available online: www.michigan.gov/firstgentleman, Reading for Leading. Access date: December 12, 2005.

CHAPTER 5

1. Catherine Fredman, "A 360-Degree Spin," *Hemispheres,* October 2005, pp. 74–77.

CHAPTER 8

1. Doris Kerns Goodwin, *Team of Rivals: The Political Genius of Abraham Lincoln* (New York: Simon & Schuster, 2005), p. xvii.

CHAPTER 10

1. M. J. Adler and W. Gorman (Eds.), *The Great Ideas: A Syntopicon of Great Books of the Western World,* Volume II (Chicago: Encyclopedia Britannica, 1952), p. 1337.

CHAPTER 12

1. Joel Barker, "Scouting the Future," 2005. Available online: www.implicationswheel.com. Access date: February 21, 2006.

CHAPTER 18

1. Peter J. Gomes, "Introduction," in Paul Tillich, *The Courage to Be* (New Haven, CT: Yale University Press, 2000), p. xxxi.
2. Rosa L. Parks with Gregory J. Reed, *Quiet Strength* (Grand Rapids, MI: Zondervan Publishing House, 1994), p. 23.
3. Parks with Reed, 1994, pp. 23–24.
4. Douglas Brinkley, *Rosa Parks* (New York: Penguin, 2000), p. 111.

Chapter 19

1. Sidney Lumet, *Making Movies* (New York: Vintage Books, 1996), p. 17.
2. The Gallup Poll, "Nurses Remain Atop Honesty and Ethics List," Princeton, NJ: Gallup News Service, December 5, 2005.

Chapter 20

1. Richard Corliss, "The Very Bad Dad," *Time,* October 10, 2005, p. 62.
2. Quoted in Richard Farson and Ralph Keyes, *Whoever Makes the Most Mistakes Wins: The Paradox of Innovation* (New York: Free Press, 2002), p. 32.
3. Timothy L. O'Brien, "Are U.S. Innovators Losing Their Competitive Edge?" *New York Times,* November 13, 2005, sec. 3, p. 1.

Chapter 21

1. David Whyte, *Crossing the Unknown Sea: Work as a Pilgrimage of Identity* (New York: Riverhead Books, 2001), p. 55.

Acknowledgments

In writing a book that revolves around the theme of legacy, we became very aware of how central family is in our lives. Family is where we seek comfort and counsel, enrichment and enjoyment, love and laughter, solace and support. The most important legacy we can leave is to our families, and while we hope our work will make a contribution to the larger community, our families are the ones to whom we offer the primary thanks for making special sacrifices so we could wander off and write. They cheered us along, even as we sometimes complained loudly about the process. They were constant examples to us of the sacrifices we have to make in order to leave a lasting legacy. We can never say often enough nor loudly enough how much we cherish their love and support.

Jim would like to offer a special thanks to Tae Kouzes, his wife, and Nicholas Lopez, his stepson. "Tae, you have reignited in me the passion for living and loving. Every day I am reminded of how profoundly lucky and fortunate I am to you for being my muse and my mentor, my playmate and my companion, my constant source of inspiration and hope. Nick, thank you for the joys of being a dad, the chance to see the world through a brand new pair of eyes, and the opportunity to learn what it means to be a leader in a whole new way. You're a very special gift to us all, and you make me very proud."

Barry would like to say a special thanks to Jackie Schmidt-Posner, his wife, and to Amanda Posner, their daughter. "Jackie, you continue to be the love of my life, sharing your experience and wisdom, and frequent reminders not only that each of us does matter, but that we're fortunate to be in a position to challenge ourselves to be that change we desire in the world. Amanda, you are our most important legacy, and you remind us about the struggles of living a life with purpose, and with zest, and also dealing enthusiastically with the mundane demands of daily existence."

With these very special people in our lives, we have lots of reasons for keeping the campfires blazing.

We've been part of the Jossey-Bass publishing family for a very long time—quickly closing in on a quarter of a century! We've seen each other through a lot of struggles and a lot of successes. We are grateful for this chance to make another contribution. We're also honored to be part of the larger Wiley family—a publisher that celebrates two hundred years in the business. Talk about a legacy! Our thanks to all members of our publishing family.

This book would never have been conceived had it not been for Susan Williams, our executive editor at Jossey-Bass. She challenged us to put our lessons down on paper and kept the faith, even when we doubted ourselves. We just want to say how grateful we are for her persistence, her encouragement, and her expertise. Rob Brandt, our assistant editor, shepherded the manuscript into production. His advice and counsel, his dedication to excellence, and his attention to detail were liberating. He made our job so much easier. Our copyeditor, Hilary Powers, helped us craft the final text and improved the reader's experience in the process. Mary Garrett, senior production editor, made sure *A Leader's Legacy* made it to the presses. Without them this book would still be a manuscript. Lisa Shannon, senior editor at Pfeiffer, another Wiley imprint, deserves our deepest appreciation for keeping the lighthouse light lit. Lisa has been our internal advocate, sponsor, strategist, tactician, and cheerleader. We can always count on her to be there when the roll is taken.

We also want to acknowledge that without you, our readers, we'd never be able to make a contribution beyond the perimeter of our immediate circle of friends and family. We greatly appreciate how you have accepted us into your organizational families, and we thank you for the opportunity to join with you in leaving this world at least a little bit better than we found it.

About the
Authors

Jim Kouzes and Barry Posner are coauthors of
the award-winning and best-selling book, *The
Leadership Challenge,* with over 1.4 million
copies sold in more than seventeen different languages.
They have coauthored more than a dozen books, including *Credibility: How Leaders Gain It and Lose It, Why People Demand It*—chosen by *Industry Week* as one of its
year's five best management books—and *Encouraging the
Heart.* Jim and Barry also developed the highly acclaimed
Leadership Practices Inventory (LPI), a 360-degree questionnaire assessing leadership behavior, which is one of
the most widely used leadership assessment instruments
in the world. More than three hundred doctoral dissertations and academic research projects have been based on
the "Five Practices of Exemplary Leadership" model.

Jim and Barry were named Management/Leadership Educators of the Year by the International Management Council and received from them the prestigious Wilbur M. McFeely Award. This honor puts them in the company of Ken Blanchard, Stephen Covey, Peter Drucker, Edward Deming, Frances Hesselbein, Lee Iacocca, Rosabeth Moss Kanter, Norman Vincent Peale, and Tom Peters, who are all past recipients of the award. In the book *Coaching for Leadership* they were listed among the nation's top leadership educators. Jim and Barry are frequent conference speakers and each has conducted leadership development programs for hundreds of organizations, including Apple, Applied Materials, ARCO, AT&T, Australia Post, Bank of America, Bose, Charles Schwab, Cisco Systems, Community Leadership Association, Conference Board of Canada, Consumers Energy, Dell Computer, Deloitte Touche, Egon Zehnder International, Federal Express, Gymboree, Hewlett-Packard, IBM, Johnson & Johnson, Kaiser Foundation Health Plans and Hospitals, Lawrence Livermore National Labs, L. L. Bean, 3M, Merck, Mervyn's, Motorola, Network Appliance, Northrop Grumman, Roche Bioscience, Siemens, Sun Microsystems, Toyota, the U.S. Postal Service, United Way, and VISA.

Jim Kouzes is a popular seminar and conference speaker who shares his insights about the leadership practices that contribute to high performance in individuals and organizations, leaving his audiences inspired with practical leadership tools and tips that they can apply at work, at home, and in their communities. Not only is he a highly regarded leadership scholar and an experienced executive, the *Wall Street Journal* has cited him as one of the twelve most requested nonuniversity executive educators in the United States.

Jim is currently an Executive Fellow at the Center for Innovation and Entrepreneurship at Santa Clara University. He previously served as president, CEO, and chairman of the Tom Peters Company (1988–1999) and prior to that led the Executive Development Center at Santa Clara University (1981–1987). Jim founded the Joint Center for Human Services Development at San Jose State University (1972–1980) and was on the staff of the School of Social Work, University of Texas. His career in training and development began in 1969 when he conducted seminars for Community Action Agency staff and volunteers in the "war on poverty" effort. Following graduation from Michigan State University (B.A. with honors in political science), he served as a Peace Corps volunteer (1967–1969). Jim also received a certificate from San Jose State University's School of Business for completion of the internship in organization development. Jim can be reached at jim@kouzesposner.com.

Barry Posner is dean of the Leavey School of Business and professor of leadership at Santa Clara University (in Silicon Valley, California), where he has received numerous teaching and innovation awards. An internationally re-nowned scholar and educator, Barry is author or coauthor of more than a hundred research and practitioner-focused articles. He currently serves on the editorial review boards for *Leadership and Organizational Development, Leadership Review,* and the *International Journal of Servant-Leadership.* Barry is a warm and engaging conference speaker and dynamic workshop facilitator.

Barry received his baccalaureate degree with honors from the University of California, Santa Barbara, in political science, his master's degree from The Ohio State University in public administration, and his doctoral degree from the University of Massachusetts, Amherst, in organizational behavior and administrative theory. Having consulted with a wide variety of public and private sector organizations around the globe, Barry currently sits on the boards of directors of Advanced Energy (NASDAQ: AEIS), the San Jose Repertory Theatre, and EMQ Family & Children Services. He has served previously on the board of the American Institute of Architects (AIA), Junior Achievement of Silicon Valley and Monterey Bay, Public Allies, Big Brothers/Big Sisters of Santa Clara County, the Center for Excellence in Non-profits, Sigma Phi Epsilon Fraternity, and several start-up companies. Barry can be reached at bposner@scu.edu.

More information about Jim and Barry, their work, and their services, can be found at their Web site: www.theleadershipchallenge.com.

Index

A Note From the Publisher

We hope that you enjoyed this new book from Jim Kouzes and Barry Posner. At this point you may be wondering, like Sergey Nikiforov, "Where do I start becoming a better leader?" If you are looking for those everyday opportunities to make a small difference in your world or if you are in need of the tools to get started or a community to keep inspired, we can help. Whether you would like to read more of the inspirational words of Jim Kouzes and Barry Posner, get some feedback on how you are doing, or implement a leadership development program within your organization, there are a variety of resources that will help as you begin or continue your leadership journey. These include:

- **Books**—Jim and Barry have written several books, including the best-selling *The Leadership Challenge* as well as *Credibility, Encouraging the Heart, Christian Reflections on The Leadership Challenge,* and *The Jossey-Bass Academic Administrator's Guide to Exemplary Leadership.*
- **Workbooks**—Jim and Barry believe that an important part of the learning process is practice, practice, practice, so they have created *The Leadership Challenge Workbook* and *The Encouraging the Heart Workbook.* These interactive tools are

designed to be used during that proverbial Monday morning when you are back at your desk, faced with a problem or situation, and would like to resolve the issue using Jim and Barry's framework.

- **Assessment**—All leaders need feedback on how they are doing if they want to improve. The *Leadership Practices Inventory (LPI)* and *LPI Online* (www.lpionline.com) is the 360-degree assessment instrument designed by Jim and Barry that has helped develop the leadership skills of nearly one million people worldwide. The *Student LPI* is also available for high school and undergraduate classroom settings.

- **Videos**—These visual aids to *The Leadership Challenge* program bring inspiring, real-life examples to the leadership development process.

- **Workshop**—*The Leadership Challenge*® *Workshop* is a unique intensive program that consistently receives rave reviews from attendees. It has served as a catalyst for profound leadership transformations in organizations of all sizes and in all industries. The program is highly interactive and stimulating. Participants experience and apply Jim and Barry's leadership model through video cases, workbook exercises, group problem-solving tasks, lectures, and outdoor action learning. Quite often we hear workshop attendees describe how *The Leadership Challenge* is more than a training event. In many cases they talk about how it changed their lives. It's a bold statement, we know, but we've watched it happen time after time, leader after leader.

Combined, these offerings truly make Jim and Barry the most trusted sources on becoming a better leader. To find out more about these products, please visit www.leadershipchallenge.com. Or if you would like to speak to a leadership consultant about bringing The Leadership Challenge to your organization or team, call toll free (866) 888-5159.